DATE DUE			
Apr 4 '73			
May 12 '76			
Dec 14 79			

PRAEGER WORLD OF ART SERIES

A HISTORY OF

American Painting

A HISTORY OF

American Painting

Matthew Baigell

PRAEGER PUBLISHERS
New York • *Washington*

BOOKS THAT MATTER

Published in the United States of America in 1971
by Praeger Publishers, Inc.
111 Fourth Avenue, New York, N.Y. 10003

Library of Congress Catalog Card Number: 70–125485

Printed in Great Britain

Contents

Preliminary Note   7

CHAPTER ONE
The First Painters   9

CHAPTER TWO
The First Sophistication   23

CHAPTER THREE
Before the Revolutionary War   45

CHAPTER FOUR
The Late Eighteenth Century   63

CHAPTER FIVE
Into the Nineteenth Century   87

CHAPTER SIX
Painting America   106

CHAPTER SEVEN
Painting at Mid-Century   128

CHAPTER EIGHT
The End of the Century   150

CHAPTER NINE
Early Twentieth-Century Realism   175

CHAPTER TEN
First Generation Modernism   194

CHAPTER ELEVEN
Between the Wars   215

CHAPTER TWELVE
To the Present   240

Notes   262

Selected Bibliography   269

List of Illustrations   272

Index   285

Preliminary Note

In this account of American painting, I ignored my biases as much as possible. I tried to reach conclusions that were based on the various sources I used rather than on my preferences and inclinations. I also tried not to write the kind of history that views American painting as misunderstood European art (Homer was all right, but he did not understand Impressionism), or the kind that waves the flag unthinkingly (Bellows was great because he never went abroad), or, especially in the later chapters, the sort that finds the culmination of American painting in a particular style.

Because American painting is so consistently flavored by the special character of particular landscapes, I tried to keep the diverse American scenery in my mind's eye. This task was made the easier because I have camped with my family throughout the country during the last few years and have seen many landscapes as they might have been seen by American painters of every period, whether on the Pacific slope or in the New York subways.

I decided to concentrate on a few painters in each period, rather than to run off a list of names, and, because of the demands a survey makes, I limited myself, whenever possible, to a consideration of movements and artists' work and avoided tracing specific influences.

I would like to thank John McCoubrey of the University of Pennsylvania, who, in a variety of ways, helped make this book possible.

I owe a special word of thanks to Roger Tarman, who pointed the way through the Bartlett Cowdrey Collection of American Art Materials at Rutgers University.

For their encouragement and tactful understanding of what had to be left out, I want to express my appreciation to Brenda Gilchrist and Ellyn Childs of Praeger Publishers. I owe Ellyn Childs a separate word of gratitude for her editorial assistance.

7

CHAPTER ONE

The First Painters

The earliest surviving American paintings date from the 1660's and 1670's. During these years, Rembrandt created his final masterpieces, Peter Lely became the leading portrait painter in aristocratic London, and Louis XIV supervised an army of craftsmen working at Versailles. These events, significant in the history of European art, are mentioned here not to throw invidious light on contemporaneous American efforts but to indicate the very different circumstances faced by artists in a new land. Permanent settlements had existed for only two or three generations, and the frontier still began at tidewater. Pennsylvania had not been settled yet. In the 1660's and 1670's, only three hundred years ago, the United States did not exist.

Nobody asked the first settlers to invent an American art, but, inevitably, we attempt to find in the first paintings intimations of subsequent developments. The paintings are, in fact, old-fashioned for their time, often weak in technique and execution, and similar in appearance except to the trained eye. But these characteristics make them no less interesting as paintings and as historical documents. They are the oldest surviving works done by the settlers, and this, in itself, is exciting.

The most important paintings of the seventeenth century were produced in New Amsterdam (after 1664, New York) and in the area of New England around Boston. The New England settlers were, for the most part, English and Puritan. Many had originally lived in the eastern shires, Norfolk, Suffolk, and Essex, a broad area with a diversified trade and one in which there had been considerable contact with the Continent. These people, primarily yeoman, tradesmen, and artisans, first came into contact with Calvinism through the Flemish settlers in England who had fled the Inquisition in the 1520's.

A century later, their religion had already assumed mature form.

The congregations had made their covenant with God, and each recognized a Biblical base for church and civil law. In the late 1620's, William Laud, then Bishop of London and later Archbishop of Canterbury, initiated a policy of repression against the Puritans. This helped convince some of them to emigrate to America in order to establish a New Jerusalem across the ocean. Believing like the Jews that they were God's chosen people, they set sail in 1630 "because we would have our posterity settled under the pure and full dispensations of the gospel, defended by rulers that should be ourselves." [1]

We should not consider the Massachusetts Bay Colony the forbidding theocracy of Nathaniel Hawthorne's imagination. Many of the early settlers were merchants who had begun their careers as London tradesmen, and William Perkins' *A Cloud of Faithful Witnesses Leading to the Heavenly Kingdom* (1631), a popular book of the time, illustrated by Biblical example the ways in which faith could lead a person to worldly success. [2] For a number of inhabitants life in the colony was a mixture of business, some pleasure, and subduing the howling wilderness outside the door, as well as adhering to God's demands.

What was the attitude of these people to art and, more specifically, to painting? They were not hostile: They were simply not very familiar with it. The most important form of easel painting in England, even in courtly circles, was portraiture. Large-scale figure and narrative paintings were not in demand, and the doctrines of the Reformation inhibited the creation of religious art. The social status of painters in England before the arrival of the Flemish artist Anthony van Dyck in 1632 was no higher than that of craftsmen. The concept of the artist as a humanist did not exist, nor were there academies of art in seventeenth-century England to promote this notion. In *An Entertainment to Queen Elizabeth* of 1598, a poet says to a painter, "So shallow are we both, that the Painter must spend his colors in lymning attires, the Poet in commending fashions." [3] And the observation sums up the situation exactly.

We may justifiably conclude, then, that the religious, largely rural, and unaristocratic Puritan attitude toward painting was one of indifference. It is almost surprising that any painting was done during the first generations of settlement. We are lucky to have the portraits.

By 1640, the population of New England was about thirty thousand persons. Perhaps itinerant portrait painters were among them, but the earliest surviving works do not appear until a generation later. Their artistic sources are threefold: first, English provincial painting, with its emphasis on linear pattern and smooth surfaces; second, the Anglo-Dutch style, domesticated in England in the early sixteenth century, in which concern for realistic likeness and volumetric handling of forms is combined with traditional English taste; and, third, though minimally, the Flemish Baroque style, with its aristocratic hauteur and flashy finish. The degree to which each style informs a particular painting is impossible to calculate, especially because the complicated history of English provincial art is as yet not clearly understood. The number of Dutch-trained artists working in the various English provinces at a given time is not easy to estimate, nor, certainly, are the intensity and scope of their influence on native talent. Because the English development is difficult to unravel, the American is still more so.

The portrait of Dr. John Clark painted just before his death in Boston in 1664 (*Ill. 1–1*) is Anglo-Dutch in character. The artist grappled with the problem of three-dimensional modeling by shading parts of the face with darker tones, and the personality of the man clearly emerges from behind the whiskers and starched neck piece. The work may have been completed in England during a visit late in Dr. Clark's life, or it may have been done by an artist trained in England who was visiting or living in Boston. In any event, it reveals the chief stylistic resources available to the English provincial artist and the continuation of English provincial art on the American side of the Atlantic.

The Anglo-Dutch style, exemplified in the portrait of Dr. Clark, was fairly common in New England, but only one person familiar with the style has emerged from anonymity. He is John Foster, a Harvard graduate whose *Richard Mather* was the first colonial portrait executed in a graphic medium. Although he was primarily a printer and a publisher, Foster also painted likenesses and, at his death, was even called a "rare Apelles." On the basis of their resemblance to his woodcut of Richard Mather, three or four other portraits have been attributed to Foster, including one thought to be of John Wheelwright (*Ill. 1–2*). With a poorly trained hand following an uncertain eye, the author of this painting tried to delineate the features of the sitter. Aware of the

1–1. ANONYMOUS, *Dr. John Clark*, ca. 1660–64.

1–2. ANONYMOUS, *John Wheelwright* (?), 1677.

12

European convention of accenting face and hands while hiding the torso in shadow, but unable to convey a more than superficial sense of the character of the sitter or of his physical existence, he exhibits mannerisms common to all eighteenth-century American artists. He could not, or did not want to, create an adequate measure of space in which his figure could exist, nor did he bring the light and dark areas or the various colors into rapport with each other. Consequently, the face and hands as well as bib and cuffs pull away from the darker surrounding sections and float, seemingly unanchored, on the surface of the painting. The light areas do not even relate to each other sufficiently to form coherent designs that would somewhat offset their isolation. In this and other early paintings, forms seem bound to the surface, and each form seems set apart by a surrounding field of different color. These are two traits that recur throughout the history of American painting.

The portraits of Dr. John Clark and John Wheelwright occupy a stylistic middle ground in seventeenth-century New England painting. To one side we might place the portraits of members of the Freake, Gibbs, and Mason families of Boston, and on the other, those paintings associated with the portrait of Captain Thomas Smith. In the former group, Anglo-Dutch realism is palpable, but it is much less emphatic than English provincial linearity and meticulous presentation of detail (*Ills. 1–3, 1–4, 1–5, and 1–6*). These works are, essentially, Elizabethan costume pieces. In another country and at an earlier time, they would have shown the sitters' rank and position. American, they reveal the sitters' immediate condition and aspirations. For example, the portrait of John Freake—commissioned in 1674—amply suggests the way a successful Boston merchant and attorney would want to be pictured.

This painting is one of a number stylistically related to portraits of the Gibbs family, and they may have been the work of a single artist. Paintings of the Mason children from about the same date are also closely related in style. In all of them, the figures are sumptuously outfitted, despite Puritan laws regulating dress, and they are shown in plain interior settings. Because modeling is minimal, contours assume great importance as a means of identifying the size and shape of the figures and the cut and substance of their clothing. Instead of emphasizing only faces and hands, the limner (or limners) has elaborated

1–3. ANONYMOUS, *John Freake,*
1674.

1–4. ANONYMOUS, *Alice Mason,*
ca. 1670.

14

1–5. ANONYMOUS, *Mrs. Elizabeth Freake and Baby Mary, ca.* 1674.

1–6. ANONYMOUS, *Margaret Gibbs,*
1670.

upon the lace and finery. Everything is emphasized, and nothing is
subordinated.

The paintings suggest a time and a place removed from Boston of
the 1670's. One wonders if the Freake, Gibbs, and Mason families were
aware of this, caring only to be recorded in their finery for posterity's
admiration, or whether they saw themselves as provincial British subjects no different from the gentry in other provinces of the home country they remembered. In any event, these works are now the most
popular seventeenth-century American paintings, the ones through
which we imagine the period and that help form our ideas of what
subsequent American primitive art should look like. Yet, they are the
works of gifted and competent artists who, although working in an
old-fashioned tradition, were able to indicate fine detail with clarity
and precision and who seem to have understood the limitations of their
style and ability quite thoroughly.

Captain Thomas Smith was a mariner who probably came to New
England around 1650, and he may have been the "Major Thomas

Smith" who received a fee from Harvard University in 1680 for painting a portrait of the Reverend William Ames. The third group of portraits is linked to his name (*Ills. 1–7 and 1–8*). In this group, Anglo-Dutch realism is modified by a familiarity with Flemish Baroque taste. Facial features are clearly marked and sharply modeled. Highlights pick out cheekbones and help to model shoulders, hands, and clothing. But these highlights are not bright enough to exist independently, and they therefore help to create an illusion of three-dimensionality not present in paintings of the other groups. Furthermore, an open window in one corner, a common Baroque device, adds a measure of space to Smith's own portrait as well as that of Major Savage. Certainly, these are the most stylistically advanced of all seventeenth-century New England portraits. They have the greatest affinity with Baroque aristocratic portraiture, and they indicate the presence of an element in New England that assumed itself to be as up-to-date as any in London.

But little more of stylistic influence than is immediately apparent should be read into these paintings. There were few artists in seventeenth-century New England and none who had had first-rate training. And what miscellaneous training they had could not help them to create a specific pattern of development for painting within a flowering New England culture. The variety of sources exhibited in these early works and the failure of a local style to develop strike a note of discontinuity and decentralization of effort that will come to characterize later periods of the nation's art.

It is unfortunate that the Puritans proscribed religious painting, for the surviving portraits provide few insights into seventeenth-century life and thought. The divines already felt threatened in religious matters at the time of the initial settlement. For example, in Anne Hutchinson's trial in 1637 for "hearing voices" and her banishment, the Puritans reaffirmed their belief in revelation through Scripture rather than through direct communion with God. There were to be no visions and no voices, nor were there to be any religious images for the congregations to observe during services. Only in the carved gravestones, with their symbolic figures of life and death and their allegorical victories of life over death, would the visual treatment of religious themes be tolerated.

1–7. CAPTAIN THOMAS SMITH, *Self-Portrait, ca.* 1690.

In New York as well as New England, portraits form the chief body of surviving works. After the Dutch purchased Manhattan Island from the Indians in 1624, a considerable number of art objects were either made there by residents or brought there by immigrants. However, no existing pictures can be convincingly dated to the years before the English captured the community in 1664. And it is really only at the turn of the century that a clear picture of New York painting begins to appear. As one would imagine, Dutch realism was a principal leaven, although, as in New England, influences from all over Western Europe are apparent.

For generations, the Duyckinck family provided the city with artists, and, of these, Gerret is the first to emerge, though hazily, from a mass of documentation. Few paintings have been firmly attributed to him. His self-portrait and portrait of his wife indicate his familiarity with Baroque prototypes as well as his inability to keep them from going literally flat (*Ills. 1–9 and 1–10*). The sharp diagonals of Mrs. Duyckinck's gown, a characteristic feature of New York painting in the next generation, give it an aristocratic sweep that is in harsh contrast

1–9. GERRET DUYCKINCK,
Self-Portrait, ca. 1700.

1–10. GERRET DUYCKINCK,
Mrs. Gerret Duyckinck,
ca. 1700.

20

to the deliberate study of her facial characteristics. An anonymous contemporary portrait of Mrs. David Provoost, which does not seem to be made up of so many diverse parts, suggests the type of straightforward realism Duyckinck and other New York painters might better have attempted (*Ill. 1–11*).

Few full-length portraits were done in the seventeenth century. The. best one, and probably the finest painting executed in the New York area during the century, is the portrait of Pieter Schuyler, completed, perhaps, while he was mayor of Albany between 1686 and 1694 or soon after (*Ill. 1–12*). The probing analysis of character, a notable feature of New York painting, emerges and despite the emphatic two-dimensionality of the figure, the vigor of the pose indicates a knowledge of Baroque sources.

1–11. ANONYMOUS, *Mrs. David Provoost, ca.* 1700.

I–12. ANONYMOUS, *Pieter Schuyler, ca.* 1690.

Most seventeenth-century American portraitists relied upon engravings after European originals for compositions, poses, and details of drapery. Only the heads were taken from life. This custom, coupled with the generally low level of artistic training, makes the essential quality and stylistic character of these works extremely difficult to assess. Half-copied, they are half-empty. Half-European, they reflect only a half of the new world in which they were made. While the earliest American literature concerned itself with the metaphoric New World of Europe's imagination and, more specifically, the New Jerusalem of the Puritan mind, the early paintings are much more superficial in content. Their origins lie less in the realities of the American settlement and more in the miscellaneous training and source material the artists were able to bring with them.

CHAPTER TWO

The First Sophistication

By 1700, the colonies had become civilized places in which to live, if one was white. Boston, New York, and Charleston could provide some of the pleasures, if not all of the graces, of European cities. Merchants developed coastal and international trade, and a class of people began to emerge that furnished the basis for an American aristocracy. In architecture, modified English town houses and manor houses appeared in one community after another, most notably in what came to be called the château country of Virginia. Paintings more nearly approximating contemporary European standards also began to appear in quantity. In artistic matters, the still loyal British subjects looked to the homeland for direction and guidance.

In New England, the Puritan hold on the minds of community leaders was effectively broken despite the Great Awakening of the 1730's and 1740's. With the lessening importance of small-town life and the rise of both cities and isolated farming areas, Puritan control of minds and manners slackened. Increasing business interests and expanding trade provided many people with a different perspective from which to view life. Anglicans, who had begun to immigrate in large numbers, brought with them cultural aspirations more cosmopolitan than those of earlier settlers. In other regions, the pattern of development was similar, though affected by local conditions. Trade, business, and the ever-expanding development of land also characterized the central and southern sections of the colonies. If the preceding seventy years had been fat ones, the next seventy certainly seemed to offer more of everything to almost everybody.

As a result of improving conditions, a number of European artists came to the colonies early in the eighteenth century, among them Henrietta Johnson (in 1705 to Charleston), Justus Englehardt Kühn (in 1711 to Annapolis), Gustavus Hesselius (in 1711 to Philadelphia), and

John Watson (in 1714 to Perth Amboy, New Jersey). During these years, a number of native artists were born. These included Nathaniel Emmons, Robert Feke, and Joseph Badger.

Because the population of the South was largely dispersed on plantations, most artistic activity was confined to the larger northeastern cities where a supportive public could be found. Even so, such activity was decentralized, reflecting no special school except a generalized European one, and it was still largely the product of an itinerant trade. Before the Revolutionary War, only John Singleton Copley is said to have made a living exclusively from painting. Artists appeared and disappeared leaving no appreciable following or school.

Yet, cumulatively, the quality of painting improved. The main thrust was toward an increased sophistication tempered by the public's insistence on realistic likenesses. But even those works reflecting cosmopolitan taste revealed a preference for precisely rendered detail and sharply defined contours, so that there was a gradient rather than a deep cleavage between primitive and professional painting. Possibly, a unique American provincial style might have developed from artistic directions suggested by the Freake, Gibbs, and Mason portraits. Instead, this style went underground as primitive art and remained there, recognized, especially in the 1930's and 1940's, when sophisticated taste saw fit to do so.

An "American look" did emerge in the eighteenth century, nevertheless. It is most apparent in the repetition of figural poses from one painting to the next. These poses were derived primarily from English mezzotints, no doubt the greatest single source of influence on American painting of the period.[1] Of the models available, the mezzotints after Sir Godfrey Kneller's paintings were the most often copied. (Kneller, a German-born artist who dominated English painting circles at that time, became, in effect, the chief instrument for transmitting to the New World the pictorial fashions of eighteenth-century England.) It should come, then, as no shock to see so many American faces perched on aristocratic bodies swathed in elegant clothing, projecting ease and contentment. Kneller, of course, could not provide models for what was raw, vigorous, and dynamic in American life and, without schools or academies, American painters were not equipped to search them out. Rather, they preferred to stay as close as possible to the tastes of London.

American copies of mezzotints altered the European originals in the following ways. Surface glitter gave way to leathery halftones. Pinpointed highlights broadened out into wider areas of light. Suggestions of an atmospheric envelope were reduced to a minimum. Detail was eliminated and features grew stiff. Foreshortening, a difficult technical achievement at best, almost vanished. Modeling was simplified so that subjects looked like puffed-up balloons rather than human beings whose flesh and clothing could yield to pressures and change appearance should the light shift. The struggle to translate the black-and-white mezzotints into colored paintings rarely produced an overall tonality that encompassed and united the forms on the canvas. Instead, colors coexisted without relating to each other. As a result, though situated in their logical places, shapes did not always appear to be anatomically connected units or elements in a coherent space.

How are we to approach these paintings? As European works, they are what they are—obvious copies. As paintings done in America, they become part of a large group having certain traits in common. As American works, they tell us more about the sources artists relied upon than what it was like to be alive in America at the time. If there is one major conclusion to be drawn from these works, it is that however much American painters might scrutinize their own landscape, they would not deny the ultimate sources of their art and culture. They saw themselves as Americans but also as Europeans in America.

Of the earliest European arrivals in America in the new century, Gustavus Hesselius is perhaps the most interesting. A native of Sweden, he settled in Philadelphia in 1712, and subsequently made one or more painting trips through Delaware, Maryland, and Virginia between 1715 and 1730, and then again around 1740. For many years, he was the most competent artist living and working in the middle colonies. If, on the basis of a handful of attributed works, we can accurately chart his artistic development, then we can recognize in them a pattern similar to that in the work of other European-born and European-trained artists. The earliest American works reflect cosmopolitan standards of portraiture while the later paintings are more realistic, less subtly modeled, and more tightly drawn. Whether these changes are based on the deterioration of Hesselius' academic technique through lack of contact with other trained painters or on the demands of his sitters for plainly wrought realistic likenesses is difficult to say. Undoubtedly, both factors are important. In 1733, James Logan, William Penn's deputy, praised Hesselius' ability to record even the facial blemishes of his masculine patrons, though he noted that women did not care to sit for him.[2] (Years later, in 1765, John Singleton Copley was to state in a letter to an English engraver who was copying one of his portraits, "I shall likewise depend on your particular care in the preservation of the likeness that being a main part of the excellency of a portrait in the opinion of our New England Conoseurs.") [3]

Whatever the reasons for the changes in Hesselius' art, they are clear to see. In *Mrs. Henry Darnall III* (*Ill. 2–1*), a painter trained in late Baroque style is at work, softening the flesh tones, allowing the gown to fall in easy folds, suggesting gauzy textures, and providing his sitter with an elegance she may well have wished she really had. Almost twenty years later, Hesselius portrayed his wife in a considerably more probing way (*Ill. 2–2*). Her skin is tautly drawn and her clothing is opaque. She emerges as a real person, a bit tired and worn, with whom one could have a conversation. She is not a fashion plate.

The range of Hesselius' subject matter provokes as much interest as his psychological growth. His *Bacchus and Ariadne* is probably the earliest colonial mythological piece (*Ill. 2–3*), and his *Last Supper,* executed for the church of St. Barnabas in Prince George's County, Maryland, in 1721, may be the first colonial religious painting. For John Penn, proprietor of the colony of Pennsylvania, he painted portraits of the Delaware Indian chiefs Tishcohan and Lapowinsa, the earliest serious (and realistic) studies of Indians by an American painter. No other painter of the time attempted such diverse themes, although John Smibert did entertain himself by painting "landscips" during his declining years in Boston. Perhaps Hesselius was prompted by the intellectual excitement of Philadelphia, certainly then the most culturally adventurous city in the colonies. In any event, of all the early eighteenth-century artists who traveled to America, he seems to have been the right one for that bustling city.

26

2–1. GUSTAVUS HESSELIUS, *Mrs. Henry Darnall III*, 1722.

2–2. GUSTAVUS HESSELIUS, *Mrs. Gustavus Hesselius, ca.* 1740.

2–3. GUSTAVUS HESSELIUS,
Bacchus and Ariadne, ca.
1720's.

2–4. CHARLES BRIDGES, *Anne
Byrd,* 1735.

2–5. CHARLES BRIDGES, *Governor Alexander Spotswood, 1735–36.*

Hesselius was one of four major painters who journeyed through the South before the Revolutionary War. The other three were his son John, John Wollaston, and Charles Bridges. Bridges was about seventy years old when he arrived in Virginia around 1735, the first professional English artist to visit that wealthy colony with a knowledge of the Kneller tradition of late Baroque elegance conveyed through formularized poses.

Despite his advanced age, he crossed the Atlantic, perhaps because of an acquaintance with the famous William Byrd II of Westover, whom he had met in England. As a result of their renewed friendship, Bridges painted members of the Byrd family as well as other important persons in the colony (*Ills. 2–4 and 2–5*). His works indicate that he would have received numerous commissions wherever he traveled. With Smibert in Boston and Hesselius in Philadelphia, he was one of the most sophisticated artists then active in the colonies. Unfortunately for subsequent painters, who might have learned as much from him as they did from Smibert, Bridges returned to England in 1740 under circumstances as mysterious as those surrounding his arrival.

29

2–6. ANONYMOUS, *Portrait of John Van Cortlandt, ca.* 1731.

In the New York area, a person wanting a portrait of himself could sit to a bewildering number of painters whose styles ranged from a reasonable approximation of Continental modes to outright amateurishness. Perhaps the most interesting are those James Thomas Flexner has called the Patroon Painters, a group of about six or seven artists who flourished in the Hudson Valley between 1715 and 1730.[4] Although attribution of works is still imprecise, individual personalities can be distinguished. One painter evokes a sense of innocence from his figures, another is purely poetic, while a third is entirely straightforward. Yet, together they make up the first coherent school of painting in the colonies. Aware of European styles through mezzotint copies but unable to imitate them accurately, they developed instead a manner notable for marvelous flat-patterned clothing enlivened by assertive diagonals and verticals, broad curving planes, and simple color combinations (*Ills. 2–6 and 2–7*). Like the paintings of the Freake, Gibbs, and Mason families, these are costume pieces. But the New Yorkers seem able to enjoy their material possessions with more gusto than the Bostonians.

2–7. ANONYMOUS, *Phila Franks (Mrs. Oliver DeLancey) and David Franks*, ca. 1735.

If it had not been for the visionary project of Dr. George Berkeley, Dean of Derry, to establish in Bermuda a college for the education and conversion of American Indians, John Smibert might never have emigrated to the colonies. The most accomplished European painter to cross the Atlantic before the Revolutionary War, Smibert had agreed to accompany Berkeley as professor of art and architecture. Despite the fact that the scheme was doomed to failure because of inadequate financing and because Bermuda was too far from the mainland, the party sailed in 1728, landing in Newport, Rhode Island, the following year.

The Scottish-born Smibert had been apprenticed to a house painter and plasterer early in life, and he probably left his native Edinburgh for London about 1709 to advance himself in the art world. There, it is thought, he studied under James Thornhill, an English late-Baroque painter. Smibert then traveled in Italy between 1717 and 1720, and after his return became one of the recognized painters of the second rank. When he journeyed to America, he brought much of the paraphernalia of an English artist's studio with him—engravings, busts, paintings, and copies of famous masterpieces, including Van Dyck's portrait head of Cardinal Bentivoglio, a painting that later provided an introduction to Venetian coloring for artists such as John Trumbull and Washington Allston. In fact, Smibert's studio became a mecca for Robert Feke, Copley, Charles Willson Peale, Trumbull, and Allston, among others, and the many paintings there served as models for the young colonials before they traveled abroad to study Smibert's own sources. Smibert himself became a model for Americans interested in a career of painting, and he probably inspired other English artists, including Charles Bridges, Joseph Blackburn, and John Wollaston, to try their luck in the colonies.

The audacious purpose that prompted Smibert's voyage to America was matched by the ambitiousness of one of the first paintings he completed on his arrival, *The Bermuda Group* (*Ill. 2–8*). This multifigured composition, which set a colonial standard for at least two generations, was Smibert's finest and most important work. Dean Berkeley stands to the right next to his wife while Smibert is at the far left. Around the turkey rug are other family members. In proper English fashion, the women look vacuous in contrast to the men, who are strongly individual. Yet, the figures seem able to communicate with each other easily, a rare achievement in American painting regardless of time or place. Smibert was also able to create garments of differently textured materials that reveal the bodies beneath them. Against a suggestively receding landscape background, he arranged a sophisticated, gently diagonal pattern of heads and hands. Clearly, this was a painting exceptional in the colonies. In his ability to manipulate shapes across a picture surface, as well as in depth, Smibert had no equal.

Smibert moved to Boston soon after landing at Newport, and during the 1730's received little competition from other portraitists there. But, like Hesselius, he gradually dropped the niceties and refinements of his earlier days, substituting for them an artisan-like attack with pigment and a simplified contouring of forms. His figures, once set behind the picture plane in a space of their own, became flat shapes laid out across the surface. Although he retained to the end his ability to idealize, he nevertheless tended to paint portraits more realistically over the years. These changes in style have been attributed variously to failing eyesight, an inability to remember what European paintings looked like, and a desire to adapt his style to what historians of the period call the "American look." [5]

His paintings of Mrs. John Erving and Mrs. Daniel Oliver (*Ills. 2–9 and 2–10*) are in his earlier manner. Both exhibit Smibert's characteristically rounded chins and jaws, pursed lips, and heavy eyelids. Neither pose is original, however. The portrait of Mrs. Oliver is composed with a mezzotint of Kneller's painting of Princess Ann in mind (*Ill. 2–11*), and Smibert's portrait of Mrs. Erving is derived from another painting of the Princess of Denmark by William Wissing. Both models were often used in the colonies: The Kneller composition also served as a basis for paintings by Joseph Badger and John Wollaston, among others (*see Ills. 2–17 and 3–3*), and both Feke and Copley made use of the Wissing pose (*see Ills. 2–15 and 3–9*). Of all the artists who drew upon the mezzotints, Smibert could best imitate the facile modeling, the gracefully suggested highlights and shadows, and the creases and folds. He best understood the principles of foreshortening, as well.

One of the significant political events that occurred during Smibert's

2–8. JOHN SMIBERT, *The Bermuda Group*, 1729.

2–9. JOHN SMIBERT, *Mrs. John Erving, ca.* 1732.

2–10. JOHN SMIBERT, *Mrs. Daniel Oliver, ca.* 1731.

2–11. After SIR GODFREY KNELLER, *Princess Ann of Denmark,* 1692.

later years was the Battle of Louisburg in 1745, which checked French influence in Canada. To honor the successful British commanders, the artist, still the reigning painter in Boston, was commissioned to complete a number of full-length and three-quarter-length portraits. Unfortunately, he did them as if by rote. Realistic heads rise from uniformed bodies that are streaked with highlights rather than modeled in the round (*Ill. 2–12*). His inability to handle full-length or nearly full-length works, early in his career and again in his late years, is woefully reflected here and helps explain why subsequent colonial artists, unable to profit from his example, had great difficulty with such portraits. Yet, even as Smibert reduces modeled areas to abrupt sections of light and dark, he reveals a mature sense of patterning. His ability to handle halftones may have diminished late in his life, but his feeling for pictorial structure remained.

It was perhaps Smibert's severe illness in 1741 that prompted Isaac Royall to ask Robert Feke to paint his family portrait (*Ill. 2–13*). Feke, who became the leading colonial portraitist of the 1740's and the best American-born painter before Copley, is still a mysterious figure. Born, evidently, around 1706 in Oyster Bay, Long Island, he may have visited Newport in 1729 where he could have seen Smibert's *The Bermuda Group*. Perhaps Feke painted his own portrait at this time, basing it on Smibert's self-portrait in the large painting. Feke may have been a mariner in the 1730's and he may have learned of the latest styles and changes in taste during trips to London. In any event, he appeared in Boston in 1741, a trained painter. In succeeding years, he is known to have traveled between Newport and Philadelphia, where he executed a number of portraits, but disappeared from view soon after 1750, perhaps going to Bermuda or the West Indies where he died.

Feke did not advertise his business in these cities as was the habit of other artists. Perhaps he did not have to. His personality was considered impressive, and he appears to have moved in the best circles, as the social position of his subjects attests. That he emphasized niceties of gesture and of apparel strongly suggests that he well understood the tastes of the leading families of the colonies. Where Smibert was able to document the colonial yearning for both pictorial realism

2–12. JOHN SMIBERT, *Sir Richard Spry, ca.* 1746.

2–13. ROBERT FEKE, *The Isaac Royall Family,* 1741.

and aristocratic mien, Feke concentrated his talents on capturing the latter.

Yet, Feke's paintings betray his colonial upbringing and lack of intimate contact with the great masterpieces of European art. No matter how hard he tried he could never achieve the easy transition from one part of the body to another and the illusion of figures situated comfortably in an atmospheric space that are commonplaces of European academic performance. But for those reasons he gives us, not European bravura but a unique and psychologically correct rendering of an American aristocracy that saw itself as British and wanted to be remembered that way. It was provincial, a little wooden, and quite polite; formal and reserved, though not shy; composed of people who had a set of steel springs reinforcing their backbone.

2–15. ROBERT FEKE, *Mrs. Josiah Martin, ca.* 1748.

2–16. ROBERT FEKE, *Portrait of General Samuel Waldo, ca. 1748–50.*

2–17. JOSEPH BADGER, *Mrs. Cassius Hunt, ca.* 1760.

2–18. ROBERT FEKE, *Portrait of Mrs. James Bowdoin II,* 1748.

To his credit, Feke had capacity for improvement. The portrait of Isaac Royall and his family, obviously based on Smibert's painting of Bishop Berkeley and his entourage, shows Feke's ability to appreciate the visual equivalent of textural differences between velvet, brocade, and other soft materials, as well as his cleverness in using large, relatively unbroken areas of color as his formal building blocks. Subsequently, he learned to suggest volume by organizing his subjects pyramidally and by the abrupt application of lighter pigments, and these lessons are evident in his work after the mid-1740's (*Ills. 2–14 and 2–15*).

Refining upon a narrow but real proficiency, Feke reached his mature style between 1748 and 1750, when he painted Brigadier General Samuel Waldo, his only known full-length portrait, and Mr. and Mrs. James Bowdoin (*Ills. 2–16 and 2–18*). So refined had his style become that he polished the character right out of his sitters' faces. By this time, Feke was learning to soften highlights and to bring up shadows so that the human form could assume an integrated anatomy in a logical space. Had he painted a few years longer, he might have created a genuine American counterpart to the Baroque portrait of fashion.

In the portraits of Joseph Badger, both fashion and realism are combined and projected in a technique that is closer to the untrained norm of most American artists (*Ills. 2–17 and 2–19*). Badger's work lies somewhere between the pattern-making of a primitive and the posed renderings of a cosmopolitan. He succeeds in neither direction, but at a mid-point of his own definition he combines the two extremes into a recognizable style, no mean feat for an eighteenth-century American painter. So well does his work combine qualities of academic training and amateurishness that a Badger painting comes readily to mind when one tries to imagine a typical colonial portrait. Although the pose of Mrs. Cassius Hunt, a favorite one of the artist's, is based on a mezzotint copy of Kneller's *Princess Ann* (*see Ill. 2–11*), it has lost most of its foreshortening; the figure no longer really sits, and the body has become pasteboard; detail is not subordinated to the whole.

In virtually every artistic generation, men like Badger have been pulled along by the Smiberts and Fekes, who established the major images and themes, and they have formed a broad American middle-

2–19. JOSEPH BADGER, *James Badger,* 1760.

ground where most artists' styles lie. In virtually every generation, one artist can be singled out as representative of this middle ground— Ralph Earl for the late eighteenth century, John Kensett for the mid- nineteenth, and Pop artists for the mid-twentieth—each responding to the current tides of taste but retaining a residual artisan spirit in his work. This spirit, important to the history of American painting (in which the dividing line between the crafts and the fine arts has never been clearly defined), has become increasingly important in recent years because of a triumph of popular taste unencumbered by upper- class strivings.

43

The period between 1700 and 1750 should not be viewed simply as a prelude to Copley. Although no one would argue that the artists who flourished then were of the first rank, it was a time when the serious practice of portrait painting commenced. Although their tastes were conservative, the painters of these fifty years were pioneers in bringing art to all sections of the colonies. Most remained simple craftsmen, but slowly they helped raise their trade to the level of a profession. Particularly in the cities, painters were accorded increasing social distinction. With a greater number of paintings available to both artist and public, standards of excellence grew more rigorous. In Boston especially, the artistic soil was rich enough to nourish a man like Copley through his early years, and elsewhere patrons who had accumulated sufficient knowledge and understanding of the arts would soon send painters like Benjamin West abroad for further study.

The period is also of interest because it offers an opportunity to observe for the first time the effects of the Atlantic crossing on artists who settled in the colonies and the sociology of art patronage. During these years, the relationship between primitive and sophisticated painting, still largely unstudied today, became a significant issue. But most important, one is able to observe the first real flowering of painting in America.

CHAPTER THREE

Before the Revolutionary War

Had there been as many art critics and art historians in the colonies as there are now in the United States, they would probably have singled out the decade of the 1750's as one of special significance and change. Benjamin West and John Singleton Copley, the two most important American painters yet born, began their careers. Smibert died in 1751, Feke disappeared about that time, and their follower Joseph Greenwood left the colonies in 1752. The Baroque-derived style of these three all but vanished with them. Of the major figures, only Badger prolonged it well into the following decade. A slightly different style replaced it, one based on the Rococo paintings of such English artists as Thomas Hudson. In comparison with earlier models, Hudson's were more animated, and the proportions of his figures were slighter. Two English artists, John Wollaston and Joseph Blackburn, introduced the new style to the colonies and were primarily responsible for its dissemination.

Wollaston brought the new fashion first to New York, in 1749, and then to Annapolis, in 1753. Later in the decade, he also visited Virginia and Philadelphia, thus becoming one of the most influential painters in the colonies outside of New England before the Revolutionary War.[1] After a trip to India, he appeared in Charleston in 1767 before leaving the country once again, presumably for England. In his travels through the colonies, he influenced Benjamin West, John Hesselius (the son of Gustavus), and Matthew Pratt, a Philadelphia-based painter who subsequently studied with Benjamin West in London. Blackburn, who painted in New England between 1753 and 1774, first influenced and then learned from Copley.

Both Wollaston and Blackburn were essentially drapery painters trained to complete the backgrounds for figures worked on by better artists. Wollaston's portrait of Mrs. William Walton (*Ill. 3-3*), com-

3–1. BENJAMIN WEST, *Thomas Mifflin as a Boy, ca.* 1758.
(slightly cropped at right)

3–2. JOHN SINGLETON COPLEY, *Mrs. Ezekiel Goldthwait,* 1770–71.

3–3. JOHN WOLLASTON, *Mrs. William Walton, ca.* 1750.

Opposite

3–4. JOSEPH BLACKBURN, *The Winslow Family,* 1757.

pleted shortly after his arrival in New York, advertised his strengths and weaknesses as well as the type of portrait his potential sitters were likely to get. His women would emerge from a glittering mass of clothing, their rather rubbery arms and shoulders supporting an inflated mask. Highlights would zigzag across their clothing to emphasize the sheen of the fancy materials. He could provide his sitters with delicate proportions, but unlike Smibert, Wollaston, good drapery painter that he was, could capture only the surface, not the substance.

It is unfortunate that Blackburn is best known for *The Winslow Family (Ill. 3–4),* for he was a better painter than Wollaston. The ability to resolve compositional problems inherent in a multifigured piece like *The Winslow Family* was beyond him, but the painting is nevertheless important because its emphasis on grace and animation at the expense of dignity and stateliness is an important feature of the new style he and Wollaston brought to America. Although Blackburn, too, painted masks rather than faces, his are more sensitively modeled and do suggest some bone structure beneath their rounded contours. In other hands, the portrait of *Mrs. Jonathan Warner (Ill.*

48

3–5), with its unimaginative pose, might have become a wooden exercise, but Blackburn was able to enhance her personality almost as elegantly as Feke and to give her a psychological presence that perhaps only Gustavus Hesselius could have equaled. Had Feke lived longer, he might have altered his style in the direction of Blackburn's more delicate one; had Copley been less talented he might well have developed a style falling somewhere between the two, and this might have become the preferred mode of New England portraiture.

Not everybody could or would pose for artists who followed European standards so closely, however. There existed a substantial market for itinerant and minimally trained painters. Their works were probably more in evidence than those of painters with greater pretensions and ability. Men like the Connecticut-born Winthrop Chandler and John Durand painted matter-of-factly, and their portraits are more naturally posed than, say, Blackburn's (*Ill. 3–6*). A handmade quality, with all the awkwardness that implies, always pervades them, and they act on our perception as objects in their own right rather than as transparent screens placed before an imaginary space. In these hard-lined,

49

3–5. JOSEPH BLACKBURN, *Mrs. Jonathan Warner, ca.* 1761.

3–6. WINTHROP CHANDLER, *Reverend Ebenezer Devotion,* 1770.

harshly colored paintings with flattened forms, one sees a continuation of the point of view that informed Badger's work. They look back to the paintings of the Freake-Gibbs-Mason limners.

This combination of cosmopolitanism and amateurishness is apparent in the early works of Copley and of Benjamin West, as well—two artists who soon outgrew the mezzotints and became major figures both in America and abroad. They belong in the company of such of their contemporaries as Jacques-Louis David and Francisco Goya who helped alter the direction of Western art. Of the two Americans, only Copley had an American career of consequence.

West and Copley developed along similar lines. Born in the same year, 1738, they became familiar with art through reading on the subject as well as through seeing actual examples. Perhaps as a result of their study and the early recognition of their own talents, both had artistic aspirations that reached beyond portraiture to include history, mythological, and landscape painting. Both saw in the role of artist a position in society higher than that usually assigned to a mere craftsman. For the colonies, this attitude was remarkable, not simply for its novelty but also because their European contemporary, Sir Joshua Reynolds, was only then raising the status of English artists to a level commensurate with that of Continental painters.

Of West's American years, little need be said. A resident of Philadelphia during the 1750's, he saw works by Hesselius, Feke, and Wollaston and developed his talents little beyond them. He manipulated color less conventionally, however: By emphasizing a single hue, his *Thomas Mifflin* (*Ill. 3-1*) became an American *Blue Boy,* in effect. And with a dim vision of the range of subject matter he was later to explore, he painted a landscape (*Ill. 3-7*). But such works are hardly preparation for his metamorphosis after he reached Europe in 1760. Despite the hagiography that he allowed to grow up around his youth —and it still clutters the view—he can hardly even be considered a zircon in the rough.

Copley, on the other hand, looked like a diamond almost from the start. His American career, some fourteen years longer than West's, is also more interesting both for its length and for its character. A complainer as well as a fighter, he cuts a more dramatic figure than West, who survived many decades of English artistic life with sanctimonious

3–7. BENJAMIN WEST, *Landscape with Cow, ca.* 1750.

3–8. JOHN SINGLETON COPLEY, *Galatea, ca.* 1754.

good cheer and propriety. West's life points to moral lessons; Copley's life, particularly his inner life, might be made into a good avant-garde movie.

Raised in a highly cultivated and creative household, Copley was exposed to as much art as any child in the colonies. In 1748, his widowed mother married the engraver Peter Pelham, whose workshop was open to the boy and, presumably, to a circle of artists that may have included Smibert, Feke, Badger, and Greenwood.

The influence of these men can be seen in Copley's early work, but before his twentieth year, he had already surpassed their aims, if not their abilities, by his determined efforts to create works of the imagination. From his readings, he must have learned that paintings of historical, religious, and mythological subjects were considered major works, while portraits were not. He doggedly prepared himself to fulfill his conception of what an artist should paint. He began to study and draw from anatomy books and to copy mythological compositions while still in his teens (*Ill. 3–8*).

Through the years of his young manhood, he debated the question of going abroad. "Was it not for preserving the resemblance of particular persons," he said of the colonies, "painting would not be known in the place. The people generally regard it no more than any other useful trade . . . like that of a Carpenter, tailor or shoe maker, not as one of the most noble Arts in the world." [2] Yet, he feared leaving Boston and his lucrative practice for the competition he knew he would face abroad. But he wanted to improve his art as well as placate his ambitions. The possibility of war with England forced his decision, and in 1774 he sailed for Europe.

With Copley, as with any artist, it is more interesting to discover his unique ability than the sources that he used. His portrait of Mrs. Joseph Mann is a case in point (*Ill. 3–9*). Although the pose is like Feke's *Mrs. James Bowdoin* (*see Ill. 2–18*), the two paintings are otherwise entirely different because Copley has structured his forms more coherently, no mean feat for a boy of fifteen. In the Copley, a line runs down the hairline on the left side of the woman's forehead to the neckbone, the white cloth between her breasts, and the necklace, firmly anchoring the major forms to each other and providing the painting with a strong vertical axis. So that this motif would not overwhelm,

3–9. JOHN SINGLETON COPLEY, *Mrs. Joseph Mann*, 1753.

Copley continued the oval pattern of the neckline into the sky, thus linking, subtly, the foreground shapes with those in the distance. As if in echo of this expanding, upward movement, there is a downward curving gesture in the vertical fold of the dress under the right arm that carries across the midriff and down beside the table.

Further manipulations of pattern that would be extraordinarily sophisticated in the work of any artist, let alone a largely self-taught teenager, can be found. They justify the term "genius" as applied to Copley. Certainly, no earlier painting in the colonies can bear such scrutiny. It was not an ordinary provincial artist who, upon seeing paintings in Europe for the first time, could say, "I find the practice of painting or rather the means by which the composition is attained easyer than I thought it had been,"[3] but a painter who instinctively understood object, color, and value placement. He might have difficulty making a pair of legs credibly support a torso or in providing a proper amount of depth for a group of figures, but these were matters of training, not of innate ability. What he was able to accomplish intuitively in the portrait of Mrs. Mann, later American artists would master only as they absorbed European sensibility by conscious effort.

Yet, Copley's work shows its American origins. His figures are usually frontal, even when their mezzotint prototypes are slightly turned. His modeling rarely leads the viewer to imagine rounded forms. Stark white collars and cuffs tend to leap out of the spaces inhabited by dresses and coats. Rarely is there a central focal point to bring together such dispersed bright areas. And no matter how aristocratic the poses (and garments) seemed to be, the realistic heads sit emphatically on top. Copley did not approach personality as if it were an apple to be polished: He probed the geography of each face for telltale signs of character, of idiosyncratic marks, as if his hands were inching across the face rather than his brush across a canvas.

Although the painting is a youthful work, the personality of Mrs. Joseph Mann emerges far more clearly than does that of Mrs. James Bowdoin in Feke's painting. Copley did not like to wander too far beyond what he could understand and observe easily, a characteristic of two other of the finest American painters, Winslow Homer and Thomas Eakins. Although Copley is not the first painter in America whose works are informed by this attitude, his are the first to demonstrate cogently its artistic and interpretive possibilities.

If we can consider this attitude characteristic of an American view of art, it becomes easier to understand the dynamics of the encounter between European art theory and American artists. When they settled in London, Copley and West learned that art should encourage moral uplift and that the artist should elevate the mind by showing the great truths and moral lessons of life. But instead of choosing generalized examples from mythology and history to demonstrate these truths and lessons as their English colleague Sir Joshua Reynolds advocated, West and Copley searched for the individual situation, the recognizable incident. Instead of painting moral truths in the guise of poetic truths, they painted datable events.

In 1755, Joseph Blackburn arrived in Boston from Newport and within a year or two, Copley absorbed what he could from the Englishman and even redirected Blackburn's style to one of greater visual accuracy (*Ill. 3-10*). Although a Rococo grace is present in Copley's works of this period, his subjects, like Theodore Atkinson, often stride

3–10. JOHN SINGLETON COPLEY, *Portrait of Theodore Atkinson, Jr.,* 1757.

vigorously across the picture surface. The textures of clothing appear natural—in the Atkinson portrait the light is absorbed by the heavy coat and reflected by the silken vest. Copley does not throw a glittering array of brushstrokes across the garments indiscriminately.

About this time, Copley, barely twenty years old, defined the stylistic path he would subsequently take. Unlike Feke, who would have followed Blackburn, Copley preferred realistic candor, as is evident in a series of husband-and-wife portraits dating from 1758, from which Blackburn's graces are eliminated. Occasionally, Copley's instinct for realism would drive him to probe far beneath the surface and return with the character of his sitter intact. His portrait of John Scollay is certainly one of the most profound that had been made in the colonies (*Ill. 3–11*).

Not content to use the same poses repeatedly, Copley experimented with different ones. He also investigated different media. The portrait of John Scollay is in pastel, a medium Copley turned to around 1757 or 1758, perhaps to teach himself to better control the application of color (always a difficulty for colonial painters: Mezzotints showed changes

of value; they could not teach the colonial artists how to manipulate color). In his *Epes Sargent (Ill. 3-12)*, Copley gnarled the right hand with thick impasto as if to make certain that in the wrinkles and crevices the man's years would be evident. The leaning pose itself reinforces the impression of age. Certainly no other colonial artist painted so many old and young people so sympathetically, adding highlights and ornaments to grace youthful energy, softening and simplifying forms to dignify the age of a sitter (*Ills. 3-2, 3-13, and 3-14*).

Within the narrow artistic world of Boston, Copley explored the possibilities of the colonial tradition to its widest extent. From familiar compositions, he was able to extract new meaning. He was well aware of his own abilities and, while grinding out portrait after portrait, he complained enough about the limits imposed upon him. But his patrons wanted portraits, and without governmental patronage or the shelter of an academy, he, like virtually all American painters, had to cater to the sensibilities and taste of his patrons if he was to survive, let alone thrive. The relationship between the American artist and the American public has always been a close but difficult one as a result.

57

3–12. JOHN SINGLETON COPLEY,
Epes Sargent, ca. 1760.

3–13. JOHN SINGLETON COPLEY,
Mrs. John Powell, 1764.

58

3–14. JOHN SINGLETON COP-
LEY, *The Royall Sisters, ca.*
1758.

3–15. JOHN SINGLETON COP-
LEY, *Portrait of Paul Re-*
vere, ca. 1768.

Needing the public, but often loathing its values, the American painter has always been uncomfortably aware of the public's presence. In each generation the story is repeated. Toward the middle of the nineteenth century, Thomas Cole said, "I am not the painter I should have been had there been a higher taste. Instead of working according to the dictates of feeling and imagination, I have painted to please others in order to exist." [4] Adolph Gottlieb spoke in the same vein, though more bitterly than Cole and most other artists, about a century later: "Having no practical or obviously useful justification, and not being tied to fundamental religious, political or social beliefs, the artist is footloose in a society which, when it does use art, usually does so on levels that to the artist are contemptible." [5]

In 1765, Copley decided to test himself against European artists and sent to London a portrait of his half-brother, Henry Pelham. On its merits, he was elected a member of the Society of Artists. Both Reynolds and West, who was in London by that time, praised the painting, but criticized its overly emphatic contours, improperly modeled color, and abundant detail. By American standards, no painting could rival this one in the subtle re-creation of personality, bulk, reflected lights, furry textures, and momentary gestures. To European eyes, it did not compose itself into a whole unified by similar tonalities, softened edges, and a central focus of interest. A portrait painted to meet these criticisms was attacked even more harshly. Sooner or later, Copley realized, he would have to go abroad. But, levelheaded to the extreme, he found it difficult to abandon his successful career in Boston.

Boston of the 1760's and 1770's was becoming a center of opposition to the English Government. Copley, however, avoided politics as much as possible, feeling that they hindered rather than aided artists. Although his father-in-law was one of the city's leading Tories, he maintained contact with both conservative and radical factions. Given his considered neutrality, it is ironic that he painted what was probably the first picture of political protest by an American artist, his *Portrait of Paul Revere (Ill. 3–15)*. The silversmith is posed in shirtsleeves holding one of his teapots, an informal and unusual pose never used elsewhere by Copley. It may have been painted in response to the Stamp Act of 1765, an act of Parliament imposing taxes on the colonies. The colonists

3–16. JOHN SINGLETON COPLEY, *Mrs. Thomas Gage*, 1771.

responded by organizing boycotts of English-made goods. In Boston, Paul Revere became one of the leading opponents of the Act. The painting, then, portraying an American craftsman holding one of his own products, might very well have been a plea to "Buy American."

Copley's paintings of the 1770's reflect an apparent awareness of the impending crisis. His figures become more grave and his color schemes darken. In a series of portraits matched only by Eakins a century later, Copley captured some of the hesitation and sense of ominousness that must have affected the public (*Ill. 3–16*). Of his portrait of Mrs. Thomas Gage, Copley said that it was the best study of a lady he had painted until that time.[6] These portraits of Tory women, less familiar today than the sturdy New Englanders, indicate that our Yankee Doodle versions of the Revolutionary War might have been passed on differently had Copley continued to paint portraits in America during the years of strife. With conflict imminent in 1774, he left the country forever.

The paintings of Copley's American career represent a tremendous achievement, because they show not only a brilliant development of insight and technical ability, but also a molding of the half-realized intentions of earlier artists into a coherent style. He was able to combine aristocratic clothing with realistic faces, making believable people, thus fulfilling both the aristocratic and realistic (perhaps, in the context of the times, democratic) inclinations of his sitters. He projected a personality into his paintings that was different from his English models. He painted an American upper class—egalitarian, on-the-make, confident of its own worth and aspirations—with a penetrating mixture of gruff observation and snobbish affection. The fact that many found themselves on opposite sides during the Revolutionary War suggests how confused must have been the cultural and social milieu he delineated with such aplomb. Not only did he often capture the psychological traits of individual clients, he also limned the sometimes complex goals of an entire generation.

Although artists including Charles Willson Peale traveled abroad and returned to the colonies before the Revolutionary War, Copley's departure for Europe marks a convenient moment to look back over the painting of the previous one hundred years. For the most part, it was confined to the larger communities, although artists visited, it would seem, almost every hamlet and plantation. The quality of American painting constantly improved, but it is impossible to point to a continuous style or a single school. Rather, the artists imitated the work of the latest European arrivals, thus ensuring a discontinuity of effort. Of those who crossed the ocean, none were first rate, and at least two Americans, Feke and Copley, were equal to any European-trained artist on American shores. European work was known at second hand by means of copies of mezzotints. These were referred to by virtually all American artists, who were thus familiar with European criteria of excellence from the start. Nevertheless, flatness, lack of a significant center of focus, sharpness of outline, and minimal manipulation of color emerge as recurring characteristics in American painting. Except in Copley's portraits, profound examination of character did not exist, nor did artists search consciously for American experiences to record. But, then, until 1776, the land was still part of the British Empire.

CHAPTER FOUR

The Late Eighteenth Century

To have been an American painter during the years of the Revolutionary War must have been an exhilarating experience. A striking new subject matter appeared—the birth of a new country. An instant history and a new set of myths had to be visualized. Noble and notable themes abounded. American artists could bask in the glory of their own new country raised to equal status with European nations. Successful in war, it was sure soon to evolve its own unique culture. The future lay in its hands. Perhaps, as many thought, America would displace England as the center of the English-speaking world, an idea occasionally discussed in eighteenth-century England and cogently expressed in the phrase of Dean Berkeley, Smibert's patron, "Westward, the course of empire makes its way." It was not, therefore, only the rhetoric of letter writing that prompted Copley to say many times that America would develop a significant school of art, one that would be recognized among the most important in the world. He was borne along on a wave of belief that many saw as a factual certainty. The waste and howling wilderness that Michael Wigglesworth had described in 1662 had become, to Timothy Dwight in 1794, the place "by heaven design'd, Th' example bright, to renovate mankind." [1]

But to painters of ambition, the prospect of national independence and the artistic fulfillment of that independence must also have been somewhat frightening. American patriots might insist that the English language was now reserved to Americans alone and that Englishmen must consequently find a new language for themselves, but American painters still required European models and European training. An American content might be found, but the vocabulary would still have to be international. Could such an art be viable, and how might it be developed? American artists lacked a structured society about which they could paint, nor did they really have an audience to address. In the 1780's and 1790's, America was still a confederation of states rather than a country with a concept of nationhood. Without such a concept to vitalize subject matter, noble themes would dissipate into individual episodes describing events rather than larger heroic ideas.

Furthermore, the artists' problems were complicated by the current notion that art was a symptom of a society living in luxury,[2] of a society perhaps on its way to frivolousness and ultimate corruption. And if art should become overly personal, it would reflect an unhealthy society in which individualism ran rampant over democracy. A temperate society required temperate art, and not too much art at that. Therefore, artists, if there had to be artists, would be wise to consider the fears of the many people and organizations that saw art as a tool of depravity. Between defining the unformed nationhood of the new country and contending with a multitude of religious, political, and historical prejudices, it is a wonder that American artists of the postwar period accomplished anything.

A generation of painters went abroad, nevertheless, to advance its art and to learn how to merge its desires and dreams with those of European artists. It is curiously inexplicable that the painters did not cross the ocean with hat in hand. Although dependent on European models when in America, some of them became examples for European artists to emulate. Two of them, West and Copley, made significant contributions to the history of European art. Gilbert Stuart mastered European conventions so well that one of his works was mistaken for a Gainsborough in later years (*see Ill. 4–10*). One may argue these facts as evidence for the poverty of contemporary English art, but they also suggest the degree to which American painters were attuned to the artistic impulses of the country as well as to the radical developments in American art necessitated by a revolutionary age. Not until the 1940's would American painters be so intimately involved with the development of European art nor so responsible for changes in its direction.

Given the disadvantage of their origin, the technical knowledge they quickly had to acquire when abroad, the competition from better-trained nationals, and the inhospitable artistic atmosphere to which some returned in America, the achievement of the Revolutionary

War generation was quite remarkable. Yet, nagging questions remain. What role did it play in American art and how did it contribute to an art in America? West left the country in 1760, and Copley departed in 1774, neither one ever to return. Stuart was abroad from 1775 to 1792. Trumbull absented himself between 1784 and 1789, 1794 and 1804, and 1808 and 1816. Ralph Earl was in England from 1778 to 1785. Only Charles Willson Peale, of those whom we consider to be the major talents of the generation, was permanently resident in the country during the 1780's, and he was a full-time entrepreneur in Philadelphia.

Was the effect of the European trips salutary or destructive? Could an artist successfully offer the lessons that he learned abroad to an American audience? Was the position an American artist could expect to hold in Europe equivalent to the one to which he would be relegated in this country? Would the subject matter appropriate in the European cultural context be easily domesticated on the other side of the ocean? If one takes into account major figures of the next generation—Washington Allston, Samuel F. B. Morse, and John Vanderlyn—the answers to these questions must be in the negative, for these men wrecked their careers on the assumption that America was ready for an art of heroic themes and noble imagery.

On the other hand, while abroad, West became a teacher to many Americans, providing them a port of entry into the stream of European art. Some, like Trumbull, Allston, and Morse, who brought back to America exalted notions about the function and nature of art as well as professionalism, helped instill in American painters (if not always American patrons) a concept of the responsibilities of art extending beyond the craft level. St. John de Crèvecoeur wrote in his *Letters From an American Farmer* (1782) that "we are the most perfect society now existing in the world." If the painters of the Revolutionary War generation did not fully realize this thought in their work, it was not for lack of trying. Abroad and at home, they did have a specific and cumulative effect on American painting, and they laid the groundwork for a viable American art that was also an intellectual discipline.

Benjamin West was the first to make an "important" painting in the European sense. When he left America, he journeyed to Rome before proceeding to London, in 1763. While in Italy, he came into contact with a group of painters and connoisseurs, including Johann Winckelmann and Anton Raphael Mengs, that was developing, primarily from classical art, a new visual style and artistic ideology. In addition to the ancients, artists such as Raphael and Poussin were also treated with reverence. This group felt that paintings should have noble themes, preferably based on history, capable of appealing to the intellect. Painterly qualities were to be suppressed in favor of linear ones. This art reflected the values of the rising middle class and affirmed faith in the ultimate perfectability of man, one of the chief postulates of the Age of Reason.

When West reached England, he soon joined the circle around King George III and Sir Joshua Reynolds (eventually becoming president of the Royal Academy when Reynolds died in 1792). The chief difference between the artistic circles of Rome and London was one of degree. Reynolds was less impressed by ancient art and was therefore even more eclectic in drawing from earlier styles. He, too, accepted academic dicta concerning appropriate subject matter. Fortunately, he and other English artists had to support themselves by painting portraits and genre scenes so that there was a healthy spread between theory and performance.

Being American, West was perhaps less inclined to accept academic theory concerning appropriate style and subject matter. After painting classical themes in a classicizing style during the 1760's (he was one of the first artists to do so), West completed a revolutionary painting, *The Death of Wolfe,* in 1770 (*Ill. 4-1*), in which Wolfe, who was killed in Canada in 1758, was portrayed in modern dress rather than in classical garb. In justification of his departure from academic canons, West invoked the principle of historical truth, pointing out that the battle in which Wolfe had perished occurred in a region unknown to the Greeks or Romans and at a time long past the zenith of their civilizations; therefore, he had painted a modern-day warrior as he might actually have fallen in battle.

In its execution, the painting was less original than in its conception. The composition is derived from the classic Baroque Pietà. The Indian strikes an exotic but familiar note as the Noble Savage, and the emotional expressions and gestures of some of the figures are chosen from the common Baroque vocabulary. Although it was not the first such portrayal, it was the first accomplished in the grand manner, and its daring was instantly acknowledged. West's popularity was assured, and in 1772 he became the royal painter of history pieces.

The range of West's subject matter was vast and included themes based on the Bible, classical literature, and Shakespeare as well as history. They whetted the artistic appetites of his American pupils. He undoubtedly advised them all many times, as he did Charles Willson Peale, that

> The art of painting has powers to dignify man by transmitting to posterity his noble actions, and his mental powers, to be viewed in those invaluable lessons of religion, love of country, and morality; such subjects are worthy of the pencil, they are worthy of being placed in view as the most instructive records to a rising generation.[3]

West advised his students to be thorough. A good draftsman, he reminded them, does not make numerous drawings but fully investigates in a single drawing the character to be developed. Perhaps it was this same dogged persistence that prompted him to explore the thematic terrain of the mysterious, the magical, and the terrific as well as

4–1. BENJAMIN WEST, *The Death of Wolfe*, 1770.

the classical and heroic. Evidently, West responded to the spine-tingling gothic horrors of Horace Walpole's novels as well as to the more profound analyses contained in the British statesman Edmund Burke's *A Philosophical Enquiry into the Origin of Our Ideas of the Sublime and Beautiful* (1757). In this book, Burke analyzed the sources of sublimity and found them in confused images, obscurity, measureless spaces, and uncontrollable power. West's *Saul and the Witch of Endor* (*Ill. 4–2*) reflects such feelings, as does *Death on the Pale Horse* (*Ill. 4–3*), a theme that West returned to more than once. Exhibited on the Continent and reproduced in engravings, it became a well-known landmark to the rising generation of European and American Romantic painters.

Like West, Copley made the grand tour before settling in England. He, too, continued to paint portraits, and explored a less broad range of subjects more intensely. His first major work completed after touring the Continent was *Watson and the Shark* (*Ill. 4–4*), in 1778. Watson, a Loyalist whom Copley knew in London, told him of a youthful encounter with a shark in Havana harbor. With an interest in geographical accuracy and the sensational aspects of the scene, Copley re-

4–2. BENJAMIN WEST, *Saul and the Witch of Endor,* 1777.

4–3. BENJAMIN WEST, *Death on the Pale Horse*, 1802.

4–4. JOHN SINGLETON COPLEY, *Watson and the Shark*, 1778.

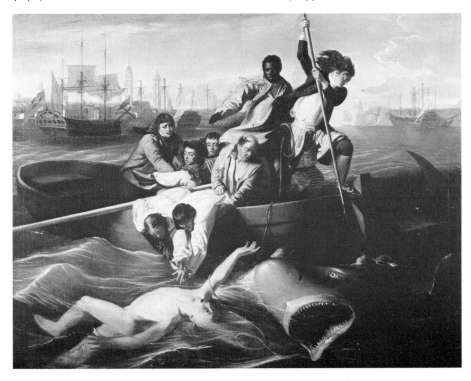

created the incident as if he were a good journalist-photographer. According to an academic canon then current, it was the artist's task to elevate the mind. But Copley's painting entertains as much as educates. With a style and an attack suggestive of the grand manner, he painted an action which had no intrinsic importance (beyond an alarming, if accurate, message about sharks).

Both West and Copley turned academic theory upside down. Instead of avoiding the specific, they searched it out. To their way of thinking, the true history painter did not concentrate on poetry or morality, but facts. Facts were exploited to the utmost in Copley's portrayal of the death of the Earl of Chatham (*Ill. 4–5*). Debating in the House of Lords in 1778 for the extension of the British war effort in America, Chatham (William Pitt) suddenly became ill and died soon after. Copley, excited by the potentialities of such an emotional scene, gathered portraits of many of those present and then arranged them in a dramatic presentation. Here, history painting became a grandiose group portrait.

Perhaps Copley was aware of his imaginative limitations. In a letter

4–5. JOHN SINGLETON COPLEY, *The Collapse of the Earl of Chatham in the House of Lords,* 1779–80.

written soon after completing the work he seems to try to justify his continued interest in portraits. He stated that they added considerably to the merit and value of his paintings. He further indicated that modern subjects were the most fitting exercise for an artist and were more likely to rouse the curiosity of his contemporaries than subjects taken from ancient history. "I have as much as possible employed myself in events that have happened in my own lifetime," he said.[4] His *Death of Major Pierson*, of 1782, and *Siege of Gibraltar*, of 1791, the latter a painting six years in the making, pictured locales, military equipment, and personnel with painstaking accuracy. Such works clearly reflect the vein of American realism that ran through Copley's English work. Head count was as important as grand, inventive gesture, it would seem. But these paintings also reflected contemporary academic theory since they depicted heroic actions. Evidently, a New England childhood and European artistic canon were not entirely irreconcilable.

It may have been Copley's friendship with emigré American Loyalists, his desire to remain on good terms with his English clientele, or his inability to create from his imagination scenes of the American Revolutionary War, but in any event his subject matter remained entirely British until he died. It fell to John Trumbull to become the painter-historian of what he termed "the noblest series of actions which have ever presented themselves in the history of man."[5] The son of a governor of Connecticut and a soldier in Washington's army from 1775 to 1777, Trumbull's thoughts about his country and his art must have become inextricably bound together by virtue of his family's interests and his own personal experience.

Encouraged by West and Thomas Jefferson, Trumbull embarked in 1786 on a plan to create a series of paintings commemorating events of the war. In these, he helped promote a new sense of American nationalism. Before the war, American history had been viewed on both sides of the Atlantic as the story of Englishmen across the ocean. Afterwards, it became identified with a new way of life, one that evoked strong feelings about the recent past as well as the potentially glorious future.[6]

From 1786 to 1797, Trumbull painted a number of small war scenes, each one including as many accurate portraits as possible. The earliest and most famous, *Battle of Bunker's Hill* (*Ill. 4-6*) and the *Death of General Montgomery*, seem to reflect the earlier rather than the later attitude toward American history, insofar as they commemorate British victories; but Trumbull soon altered his view. In a prospectus of 1790 intended to raise a public subscription for prints of the series, he wrote that the memory of scenes "in which were laid the foundation of that free government, which secures our national and individual happiness, must remain ever dear to us and to our posterity." [7]

To Trumbull, a battle had become not merely a battle, nor were the individual figures only portrait studies. They had become symbolical of feelings evoking visions of the whole struggle for American liberty. In his *General George Washington Before the Battle of Trenton*, for example, Trumbull tried to capture not the "mere map of the face," but the animating thoughts of the general before that important battle and his determined purposefulness (*Ill. 4-8*). In comparison with a similar but more mundane study of Washington by Peale (*see Ill. 4-17*), Trumbull's version, as he might have said, tried to capture the lofty thoughts and high resolve stamped on Washington's face before

4-6. JOHN TRUMBULL, *Battle of Bunker's Hill*, 1785.

the battle. Today, when such rhetoric and feelings are suspect, it is important to try to appreciate Trumbull's motivation.

Although he was a cold and exceedingly stuffy man, Trumbull infused more life into his war studies and such portraits as that of Washington than can be found in all of West and Copley. His dramatic use of color (particularly his habit of repeating coloristic accents for emotional effect) and the softened edges of his forms suggest that Trumbull had a sympathetic comprehension of the Baroque tradition that was beyond the reach of the other two. Trumbull's figures, though theatrical, react and move with greater passion and mobility than Copley's and West's.

Unfortunately, the war studies, done early in his life, marked Trumbull's artistic high-water mark. When Congress later commissioned him to reproduce some of them on the walls of the Rotunda in the Capitol (they were executed between 1818 and 1824), he fell far short of his early promise. *The Declaration of Independence, The Surrender of General Burgoyne, The Surrender of Lord Cornwallis (Ill. 4-7),* and *The Resignation of Washington* are leaden by comparison, and

4-7. JOHN TRUMBULL, *The Surrender of Lord Cornwallis at Yorktown, Virginia, 19 October, 1781,* 1824.

4–8. JOHN TRUMBULL, *General George Washington Before the Battle of Trenton,* after 1792.

reduce the action and dash of the studies to a safe trot. Apparently, by 1818 Trumbull was no longer capable of expanding his studies into large-scale compositions. But it is also true that—occasional demands for a national art notwithstanding—Americans did not want and could not support American history painting in the grand manner. There was no real market for it. Nor, evidently, was there an artist with the ability and strength of character to capture the public's imagination by producing a new and acceptable set of symbols for the young country. Despite the possibilities available to Trumbull and his colleagues, and despite their achievements, this type of success was denied to them. Perhaps Trumbull suffered for his failure more than the others since he had tried to confront the problem directly.

This generation of painters also found a public that did not respond encouragingly to painting the American landscape, even as it began to search for self-identification as a nation. Its ambivalence on this point lay partly in the fact that painters like Trumbull and Ralph Earl who attempted occasional landscapes were trained to think and paint rationally, in a way that did not reflect the American experience of the landscape or the American way of observing it. It is not surprising, therefore, that Trumbull's *View of Niagara* (*Ill. 4-9*) met with little success. To a public that viewed the American landscape as untamed, as an unknown quantity, Trumbull presented a carefully balanced painting that reinforced the eighteenth-century idea of benevolent order in the universe. To a public that was beginning to develop a habit of demanding careful identification of objects,[8] Trumbull offered generalized forms. And to a public that might just have begun to respond to a rising tide of Romantic taste, Trumbull failed to emphasize the natural marvel of Niagara Falls.

Contemporary literary accounts of the landscape were more influential. For example, William Bartram's *Travels Through North and South Carolina, Georgia, East and West Florida* . . . of 1791 had a profound effect on Wordsworth, Coleridge, Chateaubriand, and Southey, who, in turn, influenced later American painters and writers. Passages such as the one in which Bartram describes a settler "reclining on a bear-skin spread under the shade of a Live Oak, smoking his pipe, [who] rose and saluted me: 'Welcome, stranger, I am indulging in the rational dictates of nature, taking a little rest, having just come in

from the chase and fishing,' " [9] would excite the nineteenth-century taste both for the exotic and for personal communion with nature. Artists of Trumbull's generation, although anxious to record history in a modern fashion, were not yet ready to grapple with the landscape on the same terms. Only years later would a landscape style appropriate to the nineteenth century emerge, one that combined visual accuracy with an emphasis on the remote and strange and a personal viewpoint.

Such concerns hardly interested Gilbert Stuart, the major portraitist of the postwar generation (Copley, at work in England, excluded) and the finest American portraitist until Thomas Eakins. Primarily a painter of faces, he seldom extended his studies to shoulders and torsos. Only on rare occasions did he attempt a full-length portrait.

He sailed for Europe the day before the Battle of Bunker Hill, but did not begin studying with West for a year; then, however, he remained in his studio until shortly after Trumbull's arrival in England in 1780. During the 1780's, he became a major London portraitist. Considering only Sir Joshua Reynolds his superior in character analysis, contemporary critics agree that he neither enhanced his sitters with

Opposite
4–9. JOHN TRUMBULL, *View of Niagara on the British Side,* 1807.

4–10. GILBERT STUART, *The Skater,* 1782.

too much dignity nor "deviated into grace." [10] Certainly he sought the essential character of his sitters rather than their evanescent moods—their inner resources rather than their external circumstances—and, so, tended to paint less theatrically than Trumbull. It was Benjamin West who said that Stuart nailed a face to the canvas.

The masterpiece of Stuart's English years, *The Skater* (the subject was the artist's friend William Grant), shows Stuart's easy handling of light and space (*Ill. 4-10*). It has a unique vibrancy of surface that no other American of the period was able to match. Stuart refused to follow ready-made recipes for suggesting flesh tones. When still a student, he stated that he would follow no master, ancient or modern, but "find out what nature is for myself, and see her with my own eyes." [11] In his studies, he realized, unlike his fellow artists, that nature did not color in streaks. "Look at my hand," he once said, "see how the colors are mottled and mingled, yet all is clear as silver." [12]

His technical means for realizing visual insights were few but adequate. He first blocked in the large masses and then worked up specific features, eliminating the need for initial line studies. Although he found that good flesh coloring was based on the use of all colors, he did not mix them, for he wanted to see each shining through the other like blood through skin. The effect he sought was that of transparency, as if the surface of the canvas itself were alive and breathing (*Ills. 4-11, 4-12, and 4-13*).

Stuart returned to America in 1793 bringing the latest London fashions to New York, Philadelphia, Washington, and, finally, Boston, where he settled permanently in 1805. He painted his way through the business and political aristocracy of the country. Invariably, he omitted the symbols of their wealth and station, even their physical location. His portraits of George Washington, perhaps the most famous paintings by an American artist, project a man of sturdy ability, a person with charisma if not charm. One wonders whether these portraits would have been as popular had they been painted late in Stuart's career. Like Smibert, Stuart tended to harden his style and simplify his technique the older he became. His subjects became stiffer, though not necessarily wooden, and his surfaces were less mottled (*Ill. 4-14*). The portraits of Washington strike just the right balance between Stuart's earlier interest in aristocratic elegance (suggesting a Washington who

4–11. GILBERT STUART, *George Washington* (Vaughan Portrait), 1795.

4–12. GILBERT STUART, *Mrs. Thomas Lea, ca.* 1798.

4–13. GILBERT STUART, *Thomas Jefferson,* 1799.

4–14. GILBERT STUART, *Reverend William Ellery Channing, ca. 1825.*

4–15. RALPH EARL, *Roger Sherman, ca. 1775–77.*

4–16. RALPH EARL, *Portrait of Mrs. William Taylor, neé Abigail Starr, and her Child, Daniel Boardman*, 1790.

was father of the country, the king) and Stuart's subsequent desire to let unvarnished truth peep through (suggesting a Washington who was also the first republican of his time).

Ralph Earl was in many ways the antithesis of Stuart. Although he studied abroad between 1778 and 1785, he could not or would not give up his provincialism. (He even preferred to paint in the English provinces rather than in London.) Retaining an aura of the colonial limner, he brought old-fashionedness up to date. His figures could be mistaken for ancestors of Stuart's but are in fact their country cousins. Earl's paintings are known for their smooth surfaces, taut outlines, and detail that is clear and easy to read. No virtuoso with the brush (though he could capture textual effects), nor architect of spaces, Earl blocked in his masses with a good eye for abstract shapes and their relationships to each other (*Ill. 4–15 and 4–16*).

Between the 1930's and the 1950's, Earl achieved popularity with those who looked for the essence of American art. He painted like a primitive but obviously knew better. Recently, Charles Willson Peale has been attracting more interest. Peale's life and art have become increasingly relevant in an era when multimedia art forms are commonplace and artists are encouraged to collaborate with scientists. No longer viewed as jack-of-all-trades, a tinkerer with machinery who, because he explored a wide subject matter, was also considered a tinkerer in painting, Peale was a child of the late eighteenth century, an age that still explored the universe and its systems with logic and a sense of order rather than with Romantic intuition. It cannot be denied that some of his contemporaries had greater technical ability and were artistically more imaginative, but it is his willingness to explore the relationships between art and science that is important. Peale was an active participant in the Revolutionary War, a political radical, and a Deist. The chief vehicle for his myriad interests was his museum. It was established in Philadelphia in 1786 as an extension of his portrait gallery, then already four years old. Peale wanted his museum to be a world in miniature, embracing art, science, nature, and religion. Its policy was to celebrate and to expound upon their interactions and harmonious correspondences.[13] The same desire that prompted West to dress General Wolfe in contemporary clothing prompted Peale to create his museum, a much larger arena for the pursuit of truth and reason. In it he presented aspects of the biological and physical sciences as accurately as possible, even to the extent of painting backdrops for his stuffed animals. As much as anything else, the museum was a reflection of Peale's philosophy of life and that of his generation, the last one before the rise of Romanticism.

Viewed simply as a painter, Peale becomes a less interesting figure, although the range of his subjects was broad. A pupil of West between 1767 and 1769, he was one of the first Americans to recross the Atlantic with knowledge of European styles and attitudes. These he largely ignored, taking the commonsensical attitude that any person could paint if he applied himself with diligence, took nature for a guide, and did not try to overstep his limitations or reach beyond his level of training. Artistic imagination and inspiration were qualities he chose to ignore.

Yet, his work belies the prosaic insistence of his thoughts. His studies

83

4–17. CHARLES WILLSON PEALE, *George Washington (at Princeton)*, 1779.

4–18. CHARLES WILLSON PEALE, *Staircase Group*, 1795.

4–19. CHARLES WILLSON PEALE, *Exhuming the First American Mastodon,*
1806–8.

of the period's leading figures helped establish a visual pantheon of
American heroes. Within this category, he helped popularize a type of
portrait that became increasingly common in the nineteenth century—
neither a genre study nor a full-fledged history piece, it shows the
subject dominating a scene from his life (*Ill. 4–17*).

His *Staircase Group* (*Ill. 4–18*), a *trompe-l'oeil* of two of his children,
helped foster the subsequent Peale family interest in meticulously
rendered still-life painting. *Exhuming the First American Mastodon*
(*Ill. 4–19*) contributed to a general interest in American marvels and
homegrown exotica. And after learning French neoclassical brushwork
and finish from his son Rembrandt, who had studied in Paris from
1808 to 1810, the elder Peale became one of the best practitioners of
that style in the country (*Ill. 4–20*).

85

4–20. CHARLES WILLSON PEALE, *Hannah Moore Peale,* 1816.

The adaptability of Peale well symbolizes the strength of this generation. Flexible, undoctrinaire, these artists took advantage of the opportunities presented to them and developed their art in the direction in which their talents lay. They broke explosively the old colonial mold, established the profession of artist, contributed to the development of European art, set an example for later American painters, and created images that still retain their original freshness and power. Not many generations did as much.

CHAPTER FIVE

Into the Nineteenth Century

Artists who followed in the wake of West, Copley, and Trumbull—men like Washington Allston, John Vanderlyn, and Samuel F. B. Morse—faced problems that beset any group that follows a brilliant generation. They could not surpass their predecessors, and so they stumbled and fell. In personal as well as artistic matters, this was the most tragic generation of American artists. It was at home nowhere, neither in its art nor in Europe or America.

The failure of these men may in part be attributed to certain personal factors. Allston's painting *Belshazzar's Feast* became a humiliating personal tragedy when the artist, who began it in 1817, left it still uncompleted at his death in 1843. Vanderlyn misunderstood the type of subject matter Americans would like, and Morse possessed little imagination. These factors are of course related to other issues that had arisen in early nineteenth-century American artistic life. What could have been a heady time for these men became a disastrous one, and for the first time several dominant characteristics of later American artists were displayed: an inability to seize the most advanced intellectual currents of the time without repeated glances over the shoulders at the past; a preference for being observers of life rather than participants in it; a tendency to comment on situations rather than create them. And even though many preferred the spiritual emancipation they believed Europe offered, they nevertheless felt a need to defend their desire to paint in a moral and pragmatic America by swathing themselves in the clothes of gentility. The field of art became less the preserve of the adventurous personality than a garden of balm for the slightly fastidious.

But there is no reason to condemn artists for what they are not or cannot be. Allston's generation was not ready to explore a peculiarly American subject matter, despite contemporary rhetoric to the contrary.

They were not interested in the Indian, the frontier, the customs and character of American society, the American land, America as a symbol of liberty for a world in revolution or, any longer, in the Revolutionary War itself. They were concerned neither with national vanity nor national virility, or with many of the subjects that attracted contemporary writers. Instead, they were concerned with art as idea, and regarded the artist as a purveyor of ideas at an intellectual level above that of common people and common experiences. Surprised and dismayed that a high style would not root in the American soil, they nevertheless persisted in their attempts to plant it. In a fast-moving age, their rigid conception of art, matched by their political conservatism (Morse was a bigot), did not change with the times. Even in their own lifetime they were viewed as failures and came to be considered as artists whose eyes were so determinedly riveted on Europe that they lost sight of the American ground under their feet.

Whether they liked it or not, American painters could not stray too far from the taste of their public. As Alexis de Tocqueville observed in the 1830's, the will of the customer placed certain limits on the inventions of creators. Few generations complained so bitterly and adjusted so poorly to this hard fact. Nor did the artists know how to use properly the few institutions of art that were being formed. These included the short-lived Columbianum, founded in 1795 in Philadelphia to train artists and to exhibit their work, the American Academy of Fine Arts, established in New York in 1802, and the Pennsylvania Academy of the Fine Arts, established in Philadelphia in 1805. Organized and dominated by laymen rather than artists, the academies became repositories for casts of classical sculpture and occasional modern paintings rather than places of instruction and exhibition. Furthermore, the businessmen-connoisseurs believed their knowledge of art superior to that of most artists, thus ensuring their disfavor among the better trained painters.

Allston was clearly the best artist of his generation and one of the most intelligent and perhaps most articulate the country has produced. Like the author of gothic novels Charles Brockden Brown, Washington Irving, and William Ellery Channing, the popularizer of Unitarianism, a mystic, and the forerunner of Transcendentalism, Allston represents the break in point of view between the rational world of

Benjamin Franklin and of Charles Willson Peale and the new romantic one emerging around the turn of the century.

As a child in South Carolina, Allston delighted in tales of witches and hags, of the wild and the marvelous, and when he studied with West in London between 1801 and 1803, he found the latter's drama-filled paintings, such as *Death on the Pale Horse*, more to his liking than any others. Allston sought poetic rather than objective truth, an all encompassing feeling that pervades forms and colors and triumphs over the ascertainable facts of the exterior world. The artist, he came to believe, must be able to assimilate visual stimuli to his own nature and, in synthesizing inner and outer experiences, remain true to the life within himself. Allston's truth, although capable of expressing the dramatic, tended to be quiet, more at home with reverie than with bombast.

While we must agree with his biographer E. P. Richardson that Allston was one of the first American painters to imbue his work with a sense of mystery and solitude, to pioneer in the use of tonal harmonies, and to enlarge the range of subject matter, exploring landscapes, religious scenes, and literary themes as well as portraits,[1] it is more fundamental to our understanding of his art to realize that he painted states of his mind brought into harmony with his subjects. Allston believed that nothing in nature was fragmentary and wanted his paintings to reflect its harmony and interdependence of parts. Unlike Peale, who felt that the making of a work of art was a teachable (and therefore ordinary) activity, Allston gave to painting an exalted importance. He believed that talents and insights were critical factors and that a little vanity was a good thing. He thought it was reasonable to associate his name with those of Michelangelo and Raphael, two artists he revered.

In Allston's day, there was a shift from the idea that man was a fixed entity, understandable and rationally observable, to one that held human nature to be quite variable. The self began to claim increasing importance, and subjectivity became significant. Intuitively derived knowledge assumed a validity once reserved only for rationally derived knowledge. For Allston, man was less a creature of reason than of feeling, and he lived in a world of change and development. Implicit in Allston's view of the world was a respect for the profound and sympathetic interaction between man and nature. He felt that as man observed nature, in an appreciative or meditative manner, his perceptiveness and imagination would enlarge and he could achieve increasingly subtle modes of thought and feeling. In turn, as he became able to view the complexity of nature with greater understanding, he would be able to embrace still more difficult and elusive thoughts and feelings about it. Nature for Allston, then, became an educative force rather than a source of physical or intellectual enjoyment.

Allston developed his theories in his paintings as well as in poems and in his *Lectures on Art*, written primarily during the 1830's.[2] He read Romantic literature, and he was influenced particularly by Samuel Taylor Coleridge, whom he met in Rome in 1805. Coleridge once wrote that he "alone of all contemporary artists . . . seems to have been given to know what nature is—not the dead shapes, the outward *Letter* but the life of nature revealing itself to the Phaenomenon, or rather attempting to reveal itself." [3]

In order to suggest a realm of mystery lying beyond empirical knowledge, Allston was naturally drawn to exploit the expressive possibilities of color in his painting. Already impressed by English colorists, he was overwhelmed by Venetian painting when he visited the Louvre with John Vanderlyn in 1804. He later wrote that in the presence of the paintings of Titian, Veronese, and Giorgione, he "thought of nothing but the gorgeous concert of colors, or rather of the indefinite forms of pleasure . . . with which they filled the imagination," and which invited the viewer to finish the paintings. He also remarked upon that very special harmony which springs up between a sensitive viewer and a well-wrought painting. "They addressed themselves," he said of the Venetians, "not to the senses merely . . . but rather through them to that region . . . of the imagination which is supposed to be under the exclusive domination of music." He found their color "procreative in its nature, giving birth to a thousand things which the eye cannot see, and distinct from their cause." [4]

His landscapes were utterly unlike those of Trumbull. Even before the latter had painted *View of Niagara* (*see Ill. 4–9*), Allston had imaginatively re-created the sublime Swiss scenery in his *Landscape with a Lake* (*Ill. 5–1*). Hardly a document, it is rather a mood piece with a magic timelessness. A uniform tonality brings all the forms into

5–1. WASHINGTON ALLSTON, *Landscape with a Lake,* 1804.

5–2. WASHINGTON ALLSTON, *The Rising of a Thunderstorm at Sea,* 1804.

5–3. WASHINGTON ALLSTON, *Portrait of William Ellery Channing,* 1809–11.

harmony. Allston generally applied thin layers of pigment and glazes to capture the luminous surfaces he observed in Titian, as well as the feeling of space Claude Lorrain gave to his canvases (*Ill.* 5-2). As a matter of fact, Allston was known as "the American Titian" when he lived in Rome, an appellation of some significance, for the city was then a center of the dry, linear neoclassical style.

The kind of personality and mood that Allston projected into his landscapes is also manifest in his portraits. Rather than carefully express physical appearance or social condition, he tried to find the unique subjective qualities of those he painted and in so doing, he illuminated the state of their souls. After his return to America in 1808, he created the American portrait of mood, which substituted for the clear lighting of earlier portraits the mysterious gloom of Romantic feeling (*Ill.* 5-3).

Allston believed that when confronting the vastness of the universe, human powers were severely limited. When he returned to London in 1811 with Samuel F. B. Morse, he began to explore the fear and awe with which human beings react to the mysteries of the unknown. The paintings that resulted, often Biblical in theme, tend to be very general

5-4. WASHINGTON ALLSTON, *Dead Man Restored to Life by Touching the Bones of the Prophet Elisha*, 1811-13.

statements, with curiously little effect. Theatrically presented, the figures are posed like actors in a stage production (*Ill. 5-4*). In reworking the factual and ideal truths of neoclassical theory to fit the natural and imaginative truths of Romantic thought, Allston chose to ignore one of the basic characteristics of Romantic art; he did not project his own personality into works of strong emotional content as his European contemporaries were doing. This is less a criticism of Allston's work than a comment about his emotional reticence, a characteristic shared by many American artists. Of the American Romantics, only Edgar Allan Poe was really able to transfer aspects of his own personality to his characters when circumstances were highly charged.

Allston once said that a great artist like Raphael infused his own nature into his work and that "this power of infusing ones *own* life, as it were, into that which is feigned, appears to me the sole prerogative of genius" [5]; but he was so influenced by Renaissance painters, the only masters, he believed, who could make an artist great, that he kept losing his personal focus, and his work abounds with obvious quotations from Renaissance paintings. Thomas Cole once remarked of him: "His taste was pure and elevated far above that of most of his contemporaries," but his admiration for the Old Masters "led him somewhat astray. . . . His pictures . . . always reminded me of some work or school of art." [6]

Yet, Allston's personality did finally emerge in his paintings, but only after he returned to America in 1818. Usually, his powers are thought to have declined slowly until his death in 1843 because of the arid artistic climate of Boston, where he settled, and because of his tragic twenty-five-year struggle to complete the ambitious *Belshazzar's Feast* he had begun in England. But one can also view these as years in which he redirected his art, creating scenes of intimacy and reverie that reflected his temperament more equitably than the earlier more energetic works. These scenes glow as in a quiet dream, evoking nostalgic glimpses of the Italian landscape (*Ill. 5-5*). Even his so-called American views are reconstructions in a minor key of imaginary idyllic landscapes. They seem to be works filtered through the cloth of memory, rather than confrontations with living theory (*Ill. 5-6*).

Allston painted a number of solitary female figures (*Ill. 5-7*), which

5–5. WASHINGTON ALLSTON, *Moonlit Landscape,* 1819.

5–6. WASHINGTON ALLSTON, *American Scenery: Afternoon with a Southwest Haze,* 1835.

he often complemented with a poem. They are neither odalisques nor *femmes fatales* like their European sisters. Rather, they reflect sweetly on a memory or a thought. They are not the first, but they are among the best of a long line of such figures painted by American artists.

The late works, in addition to the more theatrical earlier ones, determined Allston's place among his peers. He was probably the first American to realize that through the manipulation of color and form, painting could be brought to express vague and allusive meanings beyond their immediate content. Allston did not start a school, but his example helped raise the technical standards of American painting and gave courage to other painters of inner vision, such as William Page, William Rimmer, and Robert Fuller.

No compensating factors softened the life or artistic fortunes of John Vanderlyn, whose early promise developed into a maturity of frustration and bitterness. Like some of his contemporaries, he, too, was unwilling to become merely a good portrait painter. Instead he sought in art an entrance to a world of higher meaning and value. That he did so largely through European styles and subjects—and that he hoped to

5–8. JOHN VANDERLYN, *The Death of Jane McCrea*, 1804.

find proper backing for his efforts in this country—doubly ensured his failure.

Although he was early influenced by Gilbert Stuart, with whom he briefly studied in Philadelphia between 1792 and 1794, Vanderlyn's mature style was French neoclassical in derivation. He stayed the better part of seventeen years in Paris (1796–1801, and 1803–15)—the first American painter to study there—before returning to America. So thoroughly did he digest European notions of historical composition as well as the flat colors, careful modeling, and smooth surfaces of current French art that his one great painting on an American theme became a French *tableau* rather than a piece of native history (*Ill. 5–8*). Scalped by Indians during the Revolutionary War, Jane McCrea came to fill a psychic need in the American mind as an image of the hard pilgrimage across the Atlantic and the fight for independence from the British. But in Vanderlyn's hands, she becomes part of a neoclassical frieze: a woman about to be sundered by Greco-Indian warriors. Vanderlyn's portrayal of the sleeping Ariadne abandoned by Theseus on the island of Naxos, a version of the classical sleeping Venus theme, only emphasizes his commitment to European art (*Ill. 5–9*). Had he remained in Europe, he would doubtless have become a respected member of the School of David.

When Vanderlyn returned to America in 1815, he tried to support himself by exhibiting enormous painted panoramas, a type of entertainment then popular in Paris and in England. His views of the grounds of Versailles, completed in 1819, were presented in New York City in the Rotunda, a building erected for the purpose of displaying them (*Ill. 5–10*). Hopeful of a large profit because, as a contemporary observer noted, cultivated taste was not a prerequisite for enjoyment and understanding, Vanderlyn failed in this venture. Americans evidently cared as little for his views of Europe as they did for his imaginative paintings. Panoramas, however, did become popular in the United States, particularly those that offered real topographical information about the native landscape. Through the 1830's and 1840's, they provided a notable combination of entertainment, visual instruction, and, in the terms of the day, mental gratification. Ultimately, their wide-angled technique influenced the styles of the Hudson River School painters.

5-9. JOHN VANDERLYN, *Ariadne Asleep on the Island of Naxos*, 1814.

5-10. JOHN VANDERLYN, *Versailles* (detail), 1816-19.

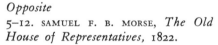

5–11. SAMUEL F. B. MORSE, *Lafayette,* 1826.

Opposite
5–12. SAMUEL F. B. MORSE, *The Old House of Representatives,* 1822.

Vanderlyn's career sputtered along until his death, but Morse's fizzled out in mid-passage. A student of Allston, his ideas of art often seem a parody of those of his master. While Allston wanted only to join the company of the Renaissance masters, Morse's ambition was "to be among those who shall revive the splendor of the fifteenth century. . . . I wish to shine, not by a light borrowed from them [Raphael, *et al.*], but to strive to shine the brightest." [7] He became enraged when thinking about the sums of money spent on what he called superfluities rather than on the cultivation of the arts. The state of art was so degraded in America, he believed, that American artists would have to emigrate if they were to receive proper patronage and support. Although he was unable to find patrons for a cultural renaissance, he did prove himself a good fighter, nevertheless. He played an instrumental role in forming the National Academy of Design in 1826, an organization set up by artists for their own benefit in opposition to the con-

servative and businessman-dominated American Academy of the Fine Arts.

As an artist, Morse had little imagination, although he was capable of occasional brilliant insight in portraiture; indeed, he helped introduce the portrait of mood to New York (*Ill. 5–11*). Riding the crest of the nationalism that prevailed after the War of 1812 and, like Trumbull, anxious to impress the Congress and obtain federal commissions, he painted *The Old House of Representatives* (*Ill. 5–12*). Its stated purpose was "not so much to give a highly finished likeness of the individuals introduced as to exhibit to the public a faithful representation of the National Hall, with its furniture and business, during the session of Congress." [8] It is true that democratic institutions, which depend on the give-and-take of committee meetings and dreary debate, do not often lend themselves to a heroic style of painting, but Morse reduced their romance yet further—to the inventory of a single, large room. He was temperamentally unable to surmount the particular and the concrete. Preferring to dream of painting impressive subjects and of obtaining commissions beyond his grasp, he grew increasingly bitter. In his forty-second year, he observed that Raphael's career had ended when

101

that artist was younger than he (Raphael had died when thirty-seven years old). By the late 1830's, Morse, realizing the futility of his interest in art, gave it up for invention and the telegraph.

Allston, Vanderlyn, and Morse all lived in Europe for lengthy periods and, when in America, were often artistically inactive. This, however, does not mean that painting came to a standstill. Rather, it indicates that the European high style could not be domesticated. Actually, there was an unprecedented amount of artistic activity in the United States through the 1790's and in the first decades of the new century. Artists of less pretension were broadening the base of American taste not only in portraiture, the staple of the artist's trade, but in still life, genre, and landscape views. In comparison with paintings of higher aspiration, the works of these men might appear meager; however, their paintings reflected more nearly the outlook and interests of the public and, in this sense, their art was more democratic. Although these artists differed in their training and in their background their paintings often share such stylistic features as taut, easily read contours, clear light that illuminates details sharply, and a simple, uncluttered presentation that is easily understood. Their point of view was, visually and intellectually, topographical. In their work, the old limner tradition was being perpetuated and enlarged. Raphaelle Peale, a son of Charles Willson Peale, expanded the possibilities of still-life painting (*Ill. 5-13*); John Lewis Krimmel of Philadelphia and Francis Guy of Baltimore and New York painted generalized scenes (rather than specific human encounters) in genre and landscape (*Ills. 5-14 and 5-15*); and Thomas Birch of Philadelphia was among the first to study carefully the special qualities of American light and to show the crispness with which it could set off forms (*Ill. 5-16*).

In the field of portraiture, the older men like Trumbull retained popularity, but younger painters such as John Wesley Jarvis and Thomas Sully, who brought portraiture to a frequently high saccharine level in Philadelphia, also commanded attention. Jarvis was an accomplished portrait painter and a leading artist in New York City after 1814. Yet his work, though highly competent, reflects the fits and starts by which American painting moved forward in the first decades of the century. For example, the advances made in his portrait of Commodore

5–13. RAPHAELLE PEALE, *After the Bath*, 1823.

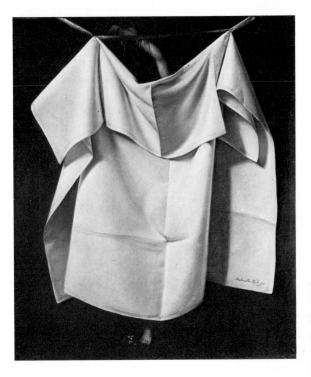

5–14. JOHN LEWIS KRIMMEL, *Interior of an American Inn*, ca. 1813.

5–15. FRANCIS GUY, *Winter Scene in Brooklyn,* 1817–20.

5–16. THOMAS BIRCH, *The "Wasp" and the "Frolick,"* 1820.

5–17. JOHN WESLEY JARVIS, *Commodore Oliver Perry at the Battle of Lake Erie,* 1816.

Oliver Hazzard Perry (*Ill. 5–17*), which so brilliantly characterizes the new type of hero that emerged in the War of 1812 (not the gentlemanly leader of the Revolutionary War, but the American equivalent of the Romantic hero, the man of action), he never turned to further account. Instead, he returned to a more sober, realistic appraisal of his sitters—one corresponding more to fact than feeling.

CHAPTER SIX

Painting America

The difference in outlook between the generation born around the turn of the century and the previous one is amazing. The artists who came to maturity during the years of Jacksonian expansion, nationalism, and reform grew up in a country that was defining itself as a nation. They were able to observe the land and its people without condescension, and they were responsive, as perhaps no other generation before or since, to the interests of the populace and to the tenor of life in the country. Their various styles emerged less as a direct result of academic training or of imitation of past masters than by direct confrontation with the objects they painted. They could even be quite critical of European art. Each artist in his own way seemed to be responding to Emerson's plea for an American Homer who would record the present. Each also seemed to reflect in his choice of subject matter the Jacksonian ideals of promoting egalitarianism and eliminating pomposity.

The new spirit of nationalism that breathed in their canvases, however, had no overtones of chauvinism, nor did their new social concern reflect blind faith in and support of the government and all American institutions. Indeed, in the paintings of John Quidor, for example, one can detect a healthy irony. Quidor's work was primarily based on themes drawn from literature, and perhaps the most famous of his paintings illustrate stories by Washington Irving (published in 1820) that offered the young nation—tongue in cheek—ready-made myths about its past. Quidor's visual interpretation, if anything, intensified the satire (*Ill. 6-1*). To laugh was one way to compensate for the lack of a set of traditions that all European countries possessed.[1]

But it was not really the American past or legend that the painters sought to capture and convey, nor even conventional European themes and styles, but the nation's present and the sense of its futurity. Few were moved by James Fenimore Cooper's lament: "There are no annals for the historian; no follies . . . for the satirists; no manners for the dramatist; no obscure fictions for the writer of romance." [2] In the work of artists like Thomas Cole and Asher B. Durand, the land itself became America's antiquity and religious testament. In the work of William Sidney Mount and George Caleb Bingham, events in the lives of ordinary people replaced noble actions and heroic ideals.

In 1824, the American critic John Neal wrote that there were only three good landscape painters in the country, Joshua Shaw, Francis Guy, and Thomas Doughty (*Ill. 6–2*).[3] Had he written his account two years later, he would certainly have added the name of Thomas Cole, whose works were discovered in a New York dealer's shop in 1825 by Trumbull. Cole, through the strength of his personality and style, helped form the first coherent school of American art, the Hudson River School of landscape painters.

That landscape painting gained ascendancy in American art in the 1830's and retained its popularity until the end of the century was not Cole's responsibility alone, of course. The image of the land itself had come to dominate the minds of Americans as well as to comprise a

6–1. JOHN QUIDOR, *Ichabod Crane Pursued by the Headless Horseman,* 1828.

substantial part of the European conception of America. Marcus Cunliffe has pointed out that nineteenth-century Americans "if challenged to produce some present sign of American greatness . . . could always . . . expatiate on nature. . . . Nature meant many things—the sheer bigness of the country, the novelty of its fauna and flora, the abundance of life, the sense of room to spare." [4] The landscape became the American equivalent of Chartres or the Colosseum. From early in the century, the study of American geography was stressed in classrooms, and as the West opened up, geography became a living entity, and the Jeffersonian agrarian ideal and the Monroe Doctrine of 1823 provided the land with a sanctity and inviolability it might not otherwise have had.

It was felt that contemplation of the landscape could provide religious instruction and moral edification. Through it, especially if it were untouched by the hand of man, Cole believed, one could more easily become acquainted with the hand of God.[5] Paintings based on the American landscape were considered fresher than any other, and were thought to be excellent vehicles for visual sermons.[6] Furthermore,

6–2. THOMAS DOUGHTY, *View of Baltimore from "Beach Hill,"* 1822.

the landscape, constant and eternal, offered solace to those confused by the encroachments of science on their once firmly held beliefs.

Nineteenth-century interest in the landscape may also have grown out of a revulsion from the noise, filth, and increasing industrialization of cities. In 1822, the first cotton mills were introduced into New England and by 1830 Lowell, Massachusetts, had five thousand factory hands. In New York, foraging pigs helped dispose of garbage. In Philadelphia in 1828, a pagoda was erected from which one could observe both urban and rural views and, as one contemporary observer suggested, ponder their meaning.

As early as the 1820's and 1830's, artists and writers alike feared that pioneer settlements would destroy the pristine features of the land. (In his novels Cooper often returned to the image of the pioneer settlement that desecrates virgin country; Cole objected to the railroad running through once wild land near his home in Catskill, New York.) Combining the nationalistic idea of America as the world's new Garden of Eden with an essentially aristocratic interest in preserving idyllic and primitive natural conditions, Cole, Durand, and their followers recorded an America seen as if for the first time, a country untouched by European sensibility, let alone settlement. Their celebration of the pure, untouched landscape was done almost in retrospect. They recorded countless unsullied prospects shortly before they disappeared completely.

Although the Transcendentalists were centered in New England and the Hudson River School painters regarded New York as their headquarters, both groups shared certain ideas about nature. "The delight which a work of art affords, seems to arise from our recognizing in it the mind that formed Nature again in active operation" [7] is a Transcendentalist thought. The purpose of art, both groups agreed, was to raise one's moral qualities and increase benevolent feelings.

One possible reason why American landscape painters began to paint increasingly larger vistas is hinted at in Emerson's essay "Thoughts on Art" (1841). He believed that artists should produce works for all men and for all time, and that their painting should become a vehicle through which the universal mind could reach the mind of mankind (rather than a vehicle for the artists' own feelings). We might infer, therefore, that a portrait of a single tree rather than of an entire forest might be too personal, too particularized, and too introspective for this universal communication. On the other hand, a panoramic view would show a vast amount and a great variety of God's handiwork, and at the same time be more impersonal. The viewer would become less aware of the artist and more of the prospect. (Interestingly, Cole and Durand criticized French Barbizon landscapes because they were too sketchy and usually contained but a few trees.)

It hardly ever rained in a Hudson River School landscape and the sun rarely set. The artists preferred the neutral light of high noon when nature was most consistent and beneficient. "In the pure blue sky is the highest sublime," Cole said. "All is deep, unbroken respose up there—voiceless, motionless, without the colours, light and shadows, and everchanging draperies of the lower earth." [8] The Hudson River artists invested the landscape with moral meaning, but in their deliberate avoidance of reading their own moods into it, they showed a remarkable lack of egocentricity. Temperamentally, their paintings lie between Allston's imaginative creations and the topographical views of men like Guy. Personal differences existed, but their work bears the unmistakable stamp of a corporate style, borne along on parallel waves of nationalism, religion, and careful observation.

Cole was the most literary and dramatic of his contemporaries. Although impressed by Doughty's landscape paintings, which he saw early in his career (in 1823) in Philadelphia (*see Ill. 6–2*), he did not follow the older man's topographical approach but chose instead to try to enlarge the possibilities of landscape painting. No "mere leaf painter," as he once insisted, he tried to mirror human experience in his moralizing, Biblical, and Virgilian landscapes as well as realistic views.

His early *Expulsion from the Garden of Eden* (*Ill. 6–3*), based on an English mezzotint by John Martin, is an imaginative re-creation of mountain grandeur and wildness. It was Cole's practice to sketch from nature, usually in the Catskill or White Mountains, and then paint his great canvases only after the particular details had receded in his mind and the essential characteristics of place and mood emerged. There are two quite contrasting moods in this work, one of tranquility in the Garden of Eden and one of the frightening and horrible life outside.

6–3. THOMAS COLE, *Expulsion from the Garden of Eden*, ca. 1827–28.

In such works, with their theatrically lit spaces and abruptly contrasting lights and darks, religious themes seem to be the vehicle for landscape studies. After Cole became a baptized Anglican in 1842, religion took precedence over nature in his paintings, and the landscape became the stage for religious themes.

But the balance is often delicately maintained. Many landscapes have a blasted tree stump in the foreground, a nature-painting device that sets off the limitless spaces beyond but which also, like a *memento mori,* suggests cycles of life and death in nature (*Ill. 6–13*). Cole brought up the color of his mountains in violation of logical atmospheric perspective so that they would seem to be living forces, growing and expanding before our eyes. His brushwork is visible and tactile, underlining the living qualities he felt abounding in nature. His surfaces were the richest yet seen in American painting. His concern for foreground detail as well as distant vista reflected his desire, perhaps need, to merge himself with the infinite.

When traveling in Europe between 1829 and 1832, Cole was able to contemplate at their source philosophical ideas he had absorbed from literature. Such ruminations lay behind subsequent sets of paintings which he called *The Course of Empire, The Departure and the Return, The Past and the Present,* and *The Voyage of Life*—works that elevated landscape to the level of historical composition and that, ultimately, dwelt on the theme of "the final nothingness of man, when acting only with reference to the things on the narrow theatre of earth." [9]

Such works mediated between European and American theory. In *The Course of Empire,* five paintings depicting the rise and fall of a nation, from its savage state to its final desolation (*Ill. 6-4*), Cole revealed his debt to a major theme in European Romantic literature, perhaps to Byron for the specific idea. [10] Yet the virtues of nature competing with the evils of civilization was also an idea explored by Emerson. The theme of luxury as a corruptive agent recurred continually in nineteenth-century American thought. Cole himself alluded in an essay to the question of whether America could alter the cycle of birth and death and save itself from the juggernaut of progress.

No doubt the scale of Cole's work was influenced by European panoramas, but its imperial breadth suggests that the vastness of the American continent was its real theater of action. In *The Architect's Dream* (*Ill. 6-5*), Cole extended buildings to infinity, in triumphant anticipation of the time "when the waters shall reflect temple, and tower, and dome, in every variety of picturesqueness and magnificence." [11]

Images evoking the past, the present, America, Europe continually reappeared in his work, invariably presented in a landscape setting. Therefore, one may regard his panoramic painting *The Oxbow* (*Ill. 6-6*) partly as a self-portrait and partly as his artistic testament. He placed an artist with his painting equipment at the lower right; the painter thus serves as the stylistic mediator, the connecting link, between the near mountainside and the distant vista. By extension, Cole and his art also become intellectual mediators between the near and far landscape, between the rain and the sun, and between the viewer and the landscape itself. If the American landscape was a new Eden, the artist saw himself holding a key of entry.

6–4. THOMAS COLE, *The Course of Empire: Desolation*, 1836.

6–5. THOMAS COLE, *The Architect's Dream*, 1840.

Asher B. Durand was a more typical Hudson River School painter. Trained as an engraver, he began to paint seriously in the mid-1830's and devoted himself steadily to landscape painting only at the end of the decade. Unlike Samuel F. B. Morse, who would not take advantage of the talents he had, Durand developed a style and an attitude based firmly on his abilities and background that gave remarkable consistency and soundness to his work. He rooted his art firmly in realistic landscape painting after briefly attempting and not succeeding at painting genre and the kind of cyclic themes Cole exploited.

His *Kindred Spirits* (*Ill. 6–7*), a painting of Cole and William Cullen Bryant done in 1849 in memory of the artist's recent death, indicates the direction of Durand's art and that of most other Hudson River School painters. Like Cole's *View of the Falls of Munda* (*Ill. 6–8*), Durand's painting is loosely organized around a vague pattern of crossed diagonals. Cole, however, filled his canvas with rich pigments and thickened forms, while Durand concentrated on suggesting the immateriality of air. Cole painted masses of trees en bloc, providing some recognizable detail. Durand denied mass by emphasizing detail.

Opposite
6–6. THOMAS COLE, *The Oxbow (the Connecticut River near Northampton),*
1836.

6–7. ASHER B. DURAND, *Kindred Spirits,* 1849.

Cole, for compositional reasons, heightened and lowered the value contrasts of different sections throughout his painting. Durand's foreground is dark and grows progressively lighter toward the horizon. He paid closer attention to atmospheric gradations than to structural organization.

Perhaps it was Durand's training as an engraver that prompted him, in one of his famous "Letters on Landscape Painting" (1855), to say that since color was difficult to control, objects should be studied in terms of lights and darks.[12] Such study, emphasizing detail and value rather than color and massing of forms, allowed atmospheric space to be clearly and evenly represented, and it carries the viewer into the pictorial space instead of detaining him in front of it (*Ill. 6-9*). By

Opposite

6–8. THOMAS COLE, *View of the Falls of Munda near Portage on the Genesee Falls, New York,* 1847.

6–9. ASHER B. DURAND, *In the Woods,* 1855.

subordinating sensuous qualities, Durand hoped that an immaterial spiritual beauty would possess each painting. Rather than impose his will on the landscape, he preferred to become an instrument to record a time and place where nature, whether in moments of calm, storm, or splendor, showed herself to best advantage.

In 1845, Durand was elected president of the National Academy of Design. At a time when Charles Baudelaire, the French poet and critic, still accepted the academic categorization of subject matter that placed landscape painting below painting based on religious, historical, and mythological themes, Durand's elevation to the post reflected the widespread approval of landscape painting in America.

Of equal importance to the enrichment of the texture and character of the nation's art was the rise of a particular type of genre painting in the 1830's and 1840's, best seen in the work of William Sidney Mount and George Caleb Bingham. While the landscape painters were raising American scenery to the level of myth, Mount and Bingham were seeking out the ordinary, everyday activities of a rural and frontier population. Earlier genre painters had gravitated toward scenes portraying wealthy people or toward studies of common people shown in a picturesque, often condescending way (just as earlier novelists like Cooper were strongly inclined to maintain social distinctions between classes and to describe common people favorably only if they were in the process of rising in the social scale). Mount and especially Bingham were profoundly egalitarian. Their attitude was not simply a reflex of Jacksonian democracy but a distinct personal willingness to observe dispassionately and accept people at their own worth. One can assume their rejection of the idea, heretofore common among artists and literati, that men should be equal in the eyes of the law but not in the assemblages of well-bred people. There is particular pertinence, then, to the idea put forth in the 1830's and still maintained in our own time that though Mount was not the first American genre painter he was nevertheless the founder of American genre painting.

After a brief stab at historical painting, he began, about 1830, to depict the rural life of his native Long Island. His interests lay neither with the abstract dignity of labor nor with the real exertions of farm life, for he evidently preferred to paint moments of relaxation and pleasure. His characters dance, play instruments, perhaps sharpen tools: They rarely labor (*Ills. 6–10 and 6–15*).

6–10. WILLIAM SIDNEY MOUNT, *Bargaining for a Horse*, 1835.

Like Durand, he found in nature the handiwork of God and was humble before it. A painting, he said should reflect spontaneous events and reveal as little as possible the work of a human hand. His figures are small in scale and do not dominate the landscape but seem to act out their lives in harmony with it. Fundamentally, his attitude was one of open-hearted accord and it extended to the painting of American blacks. Mount was one of the first American artists to do this with any regularity (*Ill. 6–11*). At a time when slavery was still acceptable, he painted them with more understanding than any of his contemporaries, emphasizing human responses to the pleasures of music and the enjoyment of leisure rather than buffoonery or the problems of slavery. (In Francis Guy's *Winter Scene in Brooklyn* [*see Ill. 5–15*], most of the working people and the man who has slipped on the ice are black.)

As a genre painter, Mount developed his own style and point of view (which are most evident in the paintings executed between 1835 and 1845), despite the potentially overwhelming influence of seven-

6–11. WILLIAM SIDNEY
MOUNT, *The Bone Player,*
1856.

Opposite
6–12. WILLIAM SIDNEY
MOUNT, *Eel Spearing at
Setauket,* 1845.

teenth-century Dutch painting and contemporary English genre painting. He rarely indulged in sentimentality nor did he usually try to tell
a specific story. Instead, he encouraged the viewer to become a silent,
living witness to the scene presented. His interiors and exteriors are
uncluttered by the residue of generations of inhabitants, and so his
figures never act in the frequently claustrophobic space of genre.
Mount's skies are bright and clearly illuminate the landscape and
figures. His desire to capture precise atmospheric effects is as keen as
that of any Hudson River School painter (*Ill. 6–12*).

A similar desire is evident in the paintings of George Caleb Bingham. Unlike the Hudson River School painters, however, Bingham
drew his subject matter from the lands around the Missouri River
and became the artistic recorder of the arrival of civilization in the
wilds. To a greater extent than any artist then living, he explored the
distinctive American way of life that developed on newly settled land.

He began seriously to record Middle Western scenes in 1844 after

returning to Missouri from Washington, D.C., where he had worked as a portraitist since 1840. Although the precise reasons for his interest in genre remain unknown, his return to his native state undoubtedly played a significant role. He may also have been influenced by a thriving regional literature, featuring stories of rivermen, backwoodsmen, and farm life that flourished in Cincinnati and St. Louis. Living in an area of intense Jacksonian democracy, he participated in politics, rising to the position of State Treasurer in the early 1860's. He painted the exercise of popular sovereignty in election scenes (*Ill. 6–14*) and, in his Missouri River boatmen, he documented the lives of those who, operating outside the established rules of civil behavior, expressed the rude egalitarianism of the West (*Ill. 6–16*). Bingham painted the recent settlers neither as heroes nor as engaging eccentrics, but as persons going about their daily activities civilizing the frontier lands.

His early *Fur Traders Descending the Missouri* set a pattern from which he rarely departed (*Ill. 6–18*). Figures are carefully highlighted and arranged so that the entire canvas can be diagrammed into circles,

6–13. THOMAS COLE, *Schroon Mountain, Adirondacks,* 1838.

6–14. GEORGE CALEB BINGHAM, *The County Election,* 1851–52.

6–15. WILLIAM SIDNEY MOUNT, *Dancing on the Barn Floor*, 1831.

pyramids, and rectangles. Drama and dash are held to a minimum. Sunlight and the ways it illuminates figures as well as the landscape are indicated by tonal variations within a narrow range of colors, rather than by abrupt color contrasts.

In *The Expulsion from the Garden of Eden* (*see Ill. 6–3*), Thomas Cole explicitly described the fear and loneliness of the solitary person in the wilderness, and these feelings are evoked in many of Cole's paintings (*see Ill. 6–13*). But this aspect of the settlers' experience was never before shown so effectively as in Bingham's *Daniel Boone Escorting a Band of Pioneers into the Western Country* (*Ill. 6–17*). Bingham could have painted the popular hero as a picturesque fugitive from civilization, the white Indian, but instead he portrayed him as the leader of a group settling the West. The scene depicted might even have come from Boone's autobiography (1784). "Over them [the mountains] nature hath formed passes less difficult than might be expected

6–16. GEORGE CALEB BINGHAM, *Raftsmen Playing Cards,* 1847.

6–17. GEORGE CALEB BINGHAM, *Daniel Boone Escorting a Band of Pioneers into the Western Country,* 1851–52.

from the view of such huge piles. The aspect of these cliffs is so wild and horrid, that it is impossible to behold them without terror." [13]

Bingham gave pictorial form to the burgeoning American myths of settlement and democracy. Interestingly enough, there was one myth he helped perpetuate by *not* painting a certain kind of subject. He did not record the arrival of industry and mechanization in the Middle West. He painted riverboatmen many times—creating a painterly equivalent of Leatherstocking, a symbol of freedom—but never the steamboat, a common sight on inland waterways as early as the 1820's. No doubt this reflected a belief in agrarianism as the ideal basis of Western life, a belief that lingered on long beyond its historical moment and was once again resurrected in the 1930's.

Bingham traveled abroad in the late 1850's, visiting Düsseldorf, which was then a popular art center. The style prevailing there influenced his subsequent painting so that his earlier straightforward reporting of ordinary sights became anecdotal illustration. In *Order No. 11* (*Ill. 6-19*), a painting that shows the effect of a military order on civilians, the stock poses, sentimentality, hard finish, and dry colors of Düsseldorf are clearly evident. This reflected one long-standing myth in American culture—that European art styles could properly record American scenes. Even so, no other artist of his generation recorded as thoroughly those experiences Europeans considered to be uniquely American.

Beyond the settlements was the open land, the frontier country inhabited by Indians. Not until Bingham's generation did artists consider the Indian as a valid subject of study, an idea that complemented the contemporary interest in the wilderness and American manners. George Catlin was among the first. Beginning in 1830, he ultimately painted over six hundred Indian pictures, many of which were reproduced in his *Letters and Notes on the Manners, Customs and Condition of the North American Indians* (1841). Impressed by the simplicity and loftiness he found in the Indian character, he believed that recording the history and customs of that race a worthy task for a lifetime (*Ill. 6-20*).

In many ways, Catlin's career points up the differences between American and European painters who were born around the century's turn. Unlike the Europeans who could turn to the past as well as a wide-ranging literature for themes and who began to develop, in the

6–18. GEORGE CALEB BINGHAM, *Fur Traders Descending the Missouri*, 1845.

6–19. GEORGE CALEB BINGHAM, *Order No. 11*, 1869–70.

1830's, the modern bohemian way of life as a means of escaping from the restraints imposed by society, Catlin had the West, the mountains, and the Indians. There was no need to rebel against civilization or government, for he could simply leave them behind. He did not have to eat his heart out, like a Byronic hero, in a mountain fastness. He could simply travel west to find either unsullied nature or the life style of another race. In these he recognized a type of knowledge his contemporaries sought: one that emanated from an uncivilized or little-civilized source. And this was considered as close to the true source of knowledge, that of a Godhood, as one could possibly get.

The American painters of this generation sought themes within the context of the nation as a whole, and celebrated shared rather than private pleasures. Their art was public in nature even if the public did not always respond to it fully. For example, even Cole's close friends indicated they would prefer his landscape scenes emptied of their historical baggage. However, the artists established a pattern of association with the public and a sensitivity to public taste that was considerably different from the increasing bohemian isolation of European artists and the greater concern for the manipulation of techniques that came to characterize European art during those years.

6–20. GEORGE CATLIN,
Big Elk, 1833.

CHAPTER SEVEN

Painting at Mid-Century

The painters who matured during the 1850's and 1860's belonged to the last generation of American artists that enjoyed widespread public esteem without suffering adverse pressure from public taste. Unlike Allston, Vanderlyn, and Morse, they were able to develop further along the lines established by their predecessors. Like their predecessors, their responsibilities to society and to their art so nearly coincided that despite complaints of misunderstanding and inattention, one may say that this period was among the pleasantest in which to have been a painter. To be sure, American painters have often been feted extravagantly, but never with such open and easy acceptance. Their popularity marked not so much America's artistic coming of age (a phrase repeated to the point of meaninglessness throughout the history of American art), but the continuing willingness of painters to base their art on societal ideals rather than abstract theories and to use art as a tool of communication rather than for the manipulation of forms and colors. And even when artists of this generation, perhaps unable to cope with the Civil War, its aftermath, and the subsequent social and industrial changes in American life, adopted European styles or singularly idiosyncratic ones of their own, they never employed a terminology that was beyond the public's comprehension.

When they wrote about art, it was to affirm the importance of nature as a teacher. This involved more than simply painting the landscape. As for Cole and Durand, it meant conveying a sense of aesthetic, spiritual completeness in a painting, uniting the simple story, the underlying message, the sentiment, and the mode of realization as the artist felt them to be in nature.

There are many ways to grasp artistic truth in a painting, but most painters of the 1850's and 1860's did so within a narrow range of expressive techniques. By and large, they and their public still preferred clarity of focus and multiplication of detail. But as the public and artists alike became more sophisticated (in part due to the dissemination of paintings and engravings through lotteries held by the Apollo Association and the American Art-Union between 1839 and 1852), American painting exhibited a greater degree of professionalism. Surfaces became more polished, landscape views became more visually exact and frequently expanded to include vast spaces, and genre detail proliferated. As the critic and historian Henry T. Tuckerman pointed out, "There is at present a love of the familiar and the highly finished in art." [1]

Familiarity was considered a basic ingredient of the art of a democratic America. Art, it was felt, should appeal directly to the people and provide them with a measure of happiness and moral elevation. Finish, however much it might show to advantage the virtues of a democratic American art, was more particularly the product of influence from the Düsseldorf School. The German city had become a mecca before mid-century, drawing artists to it such as Bingham, Eastman Johnson, Albert Bierstadt, Emanuel Leutze, Worthington Whittredge, and William Morris Hunt during the 1840's and 1850's. Its outpost in New York, the Düsseldorf Gallery, staged what amounted to a continuous exhibition of the School's artists from 1849 to 1861, when the Gallery closed.

A typical Düsseldorf School painting shown there might have had for its subject a sentimental anecdote or a historical or literary scene rendered with sentimentality. The presentation would have been quiet. In the virtuoso draftsmanship and prosaic colors, there would have been nothing suggestive or allusive, and the scene depicted would probably convey a moral.

The high and the low roads of the American Düsseldorf style are found in Leutze's *Washington Crossing the Delaware* and Richard Caton Woodville's *The Sailor's Wedding* (*Ills. 7–1 and 7–2*). Leutze, a native of Germany, lived in America from 1825 to 1840 when he left for Düsseldorf, where he remained until 1859 before returning permanently to America. Woodville was an American artist who studied in the German art center from 1845 to about 1851. In their paintings both men have indulged in voluminous detail. They have given their actors the emotional freedom to act out private dramas, thereby reducing the

7–1. EMANUEL GOTTLIEB LEUTZE, *Washington Crossing the Delaware*, 1851.

7–2. RICHARD CATON WOODVILLE, *The Sailor's Wedding*, 1852.

effect of psychological unity between them. Moreover, entry into the paintings, so generously offered by Mount and Bingham, is prevented by the tableau-like presentation. We accept the familiarity of the scenes (especially Woodville's) but we can no longer identify ourselves with them.

Though genre paintings were popular, the thoroughly American branch of painting—the historian-critic James Jackson Jarves stated—was landscape.[2] Interestingly, the very qualities of landscape that he found objectionable—literalness, a minimum of human associations, overstated atmospheric effects, a virtual failure to convey the mystery of nature—were just those qualities that appealed to a vast public much more willing than was Jarves to appreciate the different directions landscape painting was taking. These may be roughly separated in the following way: a continuation of Durand's style of Hudson River School painting; a concern for the precise notation of atmospheric effects; the development of panoramic treatment to grandiose proportions; and (primarily after the Civil War) increasingly subjective interpretation of scenes.

John Frederick Kensett, who like Durand was trained as an engraver, typifies the artists who carried the Hudson River School style into the mid-century period. Indeed, Durand and Kensett were good friends, having traveled abroad together in 1840. Unlike the older man, who remained only briefly in Europe, Kensett stayed on for seven years, living primarily in Paris and in England.

Strangely, Kensett's early paintings (those of the 1840's) do not seem to have grown logically from his training as an engraver. Impasto is thick, brushstrokes are clearly visible, and the landscape writhes—but, befitting the mid-nineteenth century, only gently (*Ill. 7-3*). By the time he returned to America, his characteristic style had become fixed. Effects of rich brushwork disappeared, and his landscapes settled into a sunny calm. Toward the end of his life, Kensett began to flatten out his views as though great horizontal sweeps of land and sea had come to dominate his vision of nature (*Ills. 7-4, 7-5, and 7-6*).

His technique might be considered an impressionism of value rather than of color change, so concerned was he with capturing aerial tones and minutely rendering the effects of light on trees, rocks, and expanses of water. In the report of an art commission to which Kensett was ap-

7-3. JOHN FREDERICK KENSETT, *English Landscape, ca.* 1843–45.

7-4. JOHN FREDERICK KENSETT, *High Bank, Genesee River,* 1857.

7–5. JOHN FREDERICK KENSETT, *Lake George,* 1869.

7–6. JOHN FREDERICK KENSETT, *Third Beach, Newport,* 1869.

133

pointed by President Buchanan are the following words, which he probably wrote:

> Bright colors are sparingly distributed throughout the natural world. The white, red, blue and yellow blossoms of plants, shrubs, and trees are not prominent even in their season of bloom: while the main masses are made up of cool greens, grays, drabs and browns intermingled, and are always harmonious and agreeable.[3]

This coincides with an observation by Henry T. Tuckerman, which may be taken as typical of the artistic vision of the period: "Nature so blends her tints as to produce a genial but not dazzling impression, which gratifies without disturbing vision." [4]

This observation, which justifies Kensett's practice of holding color effects to a minimum (so radically different from that of the Impressionists), can be easily corroborated by any person who has camped out in eastern America. Here can be found a garden, perhaps, but not a large landscape in the manner of Monet. Kensett's vision requires slightly further consideration, however. As much as he and other artists of his inclinations enjoyed the natural landscape, they saw it primarily in terms of views to be painted. Since the eastern forest was (and in places still is) exceedingly thick, no views could be found except from the heights overlooking a valley, up or down a river, or from across a lake. From these vantage points, individual colors are lost in the larger view. One thinks and sees in terms of atmospheric effects rather than of particular colors.

In Kensett's *Lake George* (*see Ill. 7-5*), for example, the relatively stable mist, a characteristic eastern mist, robs the distant forms increasingly of their color the farther away they are from the viewer. Atmospheric haze lent itself easily to Kensett's style of painting, with its concern for precise value changes, transparent depth, and smooth finish. On the other hand, one imagines that he would have failed to re-create the fogs of the Pacific Coast with the same technique because their varying textures and abrupt movements call for a more painterly and brushy treatment.

More intensely descriptive than Kensett was a large group of artists whom John I. H. Baur has called the Luminists and brought to public attention. These painters depended even less than Kensett on any sort of literary association or poetic generalization, and emphasized the observation of all objects that came into view. Broadly speaking, the Luminist style, which flourished particularly in the 1850's and 1860's, can be viewed as a continuation of the meticulous realism that informed the works of the colonial limners, Ralph Earl, and Thomas Birch, a realism that forms a kind of underground core for American painting, above which the various generational stylistic scaffoldings are built.

Luminism had no program nor even a center of operation. It appeared in many parts of the country. In the paintings of the New Englander Fitz Hugh Lane and the Pennsylvania-born peripatetic Martin Johnson Heade—its most famous exponents—the essential qualities of Luminism can be readily seen (*Ills. 7–8 and 7–7*). Usually, the sun shines at high noon on a nearly cloudless day. The air is utterly still: Movement and effort are halted, and objects, small in scale, are transfixed in a panoramic view as if seen through the wrong end of a telescope. In a short story of 1866, Henry James captured the quality of Luminist paintings: "There is a certain purity in this . . . air which I have never seen approached—a lightness, a brilliancy, a *crudity*, which allows perfect liberty of self-assertion to each individual object in the landscape." [5]

There are differences, however, between Lane and Heade. The lat-

7–7. MARTIN JOHNSON HEADE, *Lake George*, 1862.

ter's range of subject matter was broader, partly because of his wide-ranging travels. Like his younger contemporary Frederic Church, Heade journeyed to South America (in 1863–64). But instead of projecting a cosmic vision upon the landscape like Church, Heade studied minute changes of detail and color. In fact, his concern for detail is one of the hallmarks of his style. Invariably, his foregrounds contain a greater profusion of geological and floral forms than do those of Lane. Furthermore, he tended more than Lane to darken the middle distance. These stylistic habits Heade held in common with painters of the School of Düsseldorf, and since Heade spent a considerable amount of time in New York City, we may assume that he often visited the Düsseldorf Gallery and was more responsive to the works he saw there than was Kensett (*see Ills. 7–5 and 7–7*).

The techniques of Luminism, while magical in effect, are simple. Usually the sky covers fully half of the picture, and a vast expanse of water often covers most of the lower half, thus allowing a maximal amount of space in which to study reflections. The edges of forms are crisp, but never hard, so that the effect just escapes being that of cardboard cutouts. It cannot be argued that all Luminist paintings are cohesively organized, but the composition, particularly in the work of artists as good as Lane, can be incredibly subtle. In *Owl's Head, Penobscot Bay*, the diagonals of the boatman's pole, the ship's bow, the trees on the island, the island's profile, and the reflection in the water of the spit of land on the right all help to hold the composition together. At the same time, they force one's eye to follow their directional thrusts that lead to objects on the far shore and to the distant mountainscape.

From an academic point of view, the Luminists handled color quite arbitrarily (although under certain lighting conditions it may be correct): That is, the colors of the forms in the middle distance are brought up to a strength close to those in the foreground, while at the same time the far distance is grayed out. If one is to think of the near, middle, and far distances in the order of 1, 2, 3, a Luminist painting would have its colors in an order of 1, 1½, 4.

Manipulations of this sort do not occur to the same degree in the work of artists such as Cole, Durand, and Kensett—artists with a certain pretension and knowledge of European art. Rather they con-

7–8. FITZ HUGH LANE, *Owl's Head, Penobscot Bay, Maine,* 1862.

tribute to a wholly indigenous way of capturing American light and space. The Luminists found a means of dealing with the sublime size and distinctive light of the American landscape without being overwhelmed by it, and in a practical, low-pressured, even offhanded way. Far from being merely the intensely realistic end of the pendulum of landscape painting, Luminism provided the public with a fresh, matter-of-fact way to view the country's scenic wonders. Luminist paintings were, in this sense, the visual counterpart to the genre paintings of Bingham and Mount.

For a painter of ambition like Frederic Edwin Church, such simplicity was not enough. He searched for wonders in South America, the Near East, and the Arctic as well as in the United States, and he sought to re-create them with realistic accuracy and sense of poetic unity (*Ill.* 7–9). Like Walt Whitman, he tried to encompass life within the imaginative confines of his art. And just as Whitman's vision extended beyond that of nature-poets like William Cullen Bryant, whose poems can be equated with the paintings of the Hudson River School, so Church tried to reconcile more than did his contemporaries the life of art in the forms of nature.

The only pupil of Thomas Cole (between 1844 and 1846), he absorbed a largeness of conception from the older man and provided it with a firmly realistic foundation. In contrast with Cole's subjective interpretations, however, Church let the landscape announce its own qualities. By a remarkable transference of power, he let the landscape become a vehicle for itself rather than for him.

He was in part influenced by his reading of *Kosmos,* a multivolume *summa* of fact and idea by the physical scientist Alexander von Humboldt (published from 1849 to 1858). *Kosmos* offered "not only a graphic description, but an imaginative conception of the physical world—which would support generalization by details and dignify details by generalization." [6] Humboldt believed that art would flourish brilliantly if painters would concentrate upon the most varied and luxurious features of nature, and these, he thought, were to be found in the Andes Mountains and Amazon basin. His book inspired

7–9. FREDERIC EDWIN CHURCH, *Floating Icebergs,* 1859.

7–10. FREDERIC EDWIN CHURCH, *Cotopaxi, ca.* 1863.

7–11. FREDERIC EDWIN CHURCH, *Twilight in the Wilderness,* 1860.

Church to travel twice to South America, in 1853 and 1857. The paintings that reflect these trips show jungle and mountain terrains, exotic tree and rock formations, and the flora appropriate to different elevations; even more basically, they hint at the earth itself still in process of formation (*Ill. 7–10*). With only slightly less fervor did he approach scenery from other parts of the world. His *Twilight in the Wilderness* (*Ill. 7–11*) may be his finest interpretation of the American landscape.[7] In it, an uncorrupted nature completes its daily cycle untouched by human existence.

The interest in visually and physically large paintings gained momentum when American artists began to record the vast spaces of the Rockies and Sierras. During the troubled 1850's and 1860's, these mountains also helped to revitalize the myth of America as the new Garden of Eden, for they were beyond the geographical areas of conflict and industrial despoliation but were nevertheless still part of the American continent. So overwhelming was scenery of the Far West that one can well imagine why Albert Bierstadt became its most popular interpreter. He domesticated it, reduced it to the size of a living-room wall by adding genre elements, exploiting its picturesque aspects, and dramatically manipulating lighting contrasts (*Ill. 7–12*).

In the years following the Civil War, younger artists were less attracted to the Hudson River School and its variations. Painters had explored and recorded most of the land, and by the time Bierstadt had exhibited his views in the 1860's, the artistic frontier in the West may be said to have closed. Further description of the landscape would have been tiresome. Scientific pursuits also began to undermine earlier attitudes. Meticulous realism in painting became less a simple expression of reverence for God's handiwork and more an intellectual exercise— the categorization and classification of floral species and rock formations. Coupled with these general shifts in mood was a growing disenchantment with the Düsseldorf manner and a rising interest in French painting. This fact was noted as early as 1864;[8] indeed, William Morris Hunt had already returned to New England in 1855 or 1856 after a lengthy stay in France, bringing with him a style and an attitude derived from the Barbizon painters, whom he knew personally and whose works he helped popularize in this country (*Ill. 7–13*).

7–12. ALBERT BIERSTADT, *The Rocky Mountains,* 1863.

7–13. WILLIAM MORRIS HUNT, *The Little Gleaner,* 1854.

141

In face of the determined materialism that characterized American life in the post–Civil War decades, artists were faced with a choice: They could either perpetuate older styles; capitulate to the taste of the newly rich, providing them with paintings in which sentiment became sentimentality; escape into a mystical world of art or religion; or somehow accede to the demands of clients while maintaining a sense of artistic equilibrium. The responses were varied, and no single choice seems to have dominated. Although many painters flourished, two stand out as having best surmounted the difficulties and confusions of the time. They are Eastman Johnson and George Inness.

Johnson is particularly representative of the period because he painted genre scenes and landscapes as well as portraits, and because his various changes of style follow no especially evolutionary path. Furthermore, in his European travels from 1849 to 1855, he studied in

7–14. EASTMAN JOHNSON, *Old Kentucky Home,* 1859.

Düsseldorf, The Hague (where he fell under the spell of Rembrandt), and in Paris. A thoroughgoing eclectic, he translated into American terms the lessons he learned abroad.

In his most popular picture, he applied the Düsseldorf style to a Dutch seventeenth-century courtyard scene (*Ill. 7–14*). Actually, the setting was the backyard of his father's house in Washington, D.C. Like most of his contemporaries, he managed to find wholesome delight in scenes (even in his Civil War paintings) that innocently but completely missed the underlying problems that provoked the scenes in question. As Johnson obviously realized, turning a moan into a gentle sigh was a chief requisite of genre painting during those years.

Old Kentucky Home may have been based on "The Hireling and the Slave," by William Grayson. The poem was published in 1854 and purported to show the superiority of southern bondage to northern

7–15. EASTMAN JOHNSON, *The Nantucket School of Philosophy*, 1887.

wage slavery. It was a part of a spate of pro-slavery literature that appeared as a result of the success of *Uncle Tom's Cabin* (1852). In the poem Grayson describes scenes that are very like Johnson's painting.

> The cabin home, not comfortless, though rude,
> Light daily labor, and abundant food,
> The sturdy health that temperate habits yield,
> The cheerful song that rings in every field,
> The long, loud laugh, that freemen seldom share. . . .[9]

In this later age when we can assume that artists are concerned about if not personally involved with social problems, paintings such as Johnson's are difficult to fathom. He lived, however, at a time before American artists had adopted the bohemian attitude or the social militancy then just developing in Paris. His values were still those of the mainstream of society, and it would be fatuous to hold them against him. In his last important genre painting, *The Nantucket School of Philosophy* (*Ill. 7–15*), he is able to portray, with apparent ease, the ruminations of old men as if he were an intimate part of their lives. His sympathies lie clearly with them, and even though they are old, they reflect the promise and pleasantness many still found in American life.

In the 1870's, while summering at Nantucket, Johnson painted many works in a brushy style with vigorous lights and abrupt shadows. Most were studies, it is true, rather than finished paintings, but they all reveal unmistakable French influences closer to Barbizon than Impressionist sources (*Ill. 7–16*). Surfaces are rich, and studio lighting has picked out the figures from vaguely indicated backgrounds. Masses are blocked in firmly, not lost in a maze of detail. Tonal studies of mood rather than visual description, they are indicators of a change taking place in American taste.

In the same decade, George Inness was evolving a personal style based on the same sources with the forms more vaporously modeled and with edges further blurred. Although he, too, strove to have his paintings reflect high moral purpose and to be unified in sentiment, subject, and effect, his results were considerably different from those of Kensett, Church, or Johnson. Although he moved with the artistic tides of the postwar decades, he never achieved the popularity of these men

7–16. EASTMAN JOHNSON, *Woman on a Hill, ca.* 1870.

during his own lifetime; yet he was artistically more important, if only because he demonstrated so effectively the way in which the new interest in subjective values could replace the older concern for descriptive detail. Inness' development, from the Hudson River School manner of his early landscapes to his later subjectivism, was abetted by firsthand knowledge of the intimate scale and poetic appeal of Barbizon painting, with which he became familiar during numerous trips abroad between 1850 and 1875, and by this interest in the religious views of the Swedish philosopher Emanuel Swedenborg.

Cole used nature as a vessel for his emotions and Church let nature speak for itself, but Inness endeavored almost from the first actually to become a part of nature's fabric. "Under the impulse of a sympathetic feeling, [I would] put something on canvas more or less like what I was aiming at," he once said.[10] On occasion, he identified himself with objects in nature, for example, a cloud.

Soon will we join ourselves in softened forms,
And, far extended on thy horizon, lie stretched in sweep [sic] repose. . . .[11]

To Inness, the true functions of art were, first, to refine the artist's own spiritual nature and, second, to affect the spirit of mankind. This attitude, different from those of Church and Johnson, reflected the increasing alienation American artists were beginning to feel and Inness' own intense religious beliefs. His desire to raise the subjective quotient in his art caused him, in the mid-1850's, to modify his earlier work (*Ill. 7–17*): to soften the detail, to limit the physical scope of his landscapes, and to use color more freely (*Ills. 7–18 and 7–19*). Space additionally contracted as his colors tended to clot on the picture surface (*see Ill. 7–18*). He modeled forms with less vigor, omitted detail, and ignored atmospheric light as he became, in contrast to Kensett, more concerned with large, often brightly lit masses (*Ill. 7–20, and see Ill. 7–4*).

As a follower of Swedenborg, Inness believed that there emanated from God a divine sphere which, for example, manifested itself in the spiritual world as a spiritual sun, which in turn was reflected in the sun of the natural world. Perhaps the hazy skies of his late paintings, with their elusive suns and impending storms, reflect his desire to

7-17. GEORGE INNESS, *The Sun Shower*, 1847.

7-18. GEORGE INNESS, *Autumn Landscape, October*, 1886.

penetrate the mysteries of the natural and spiritual worlds. On the other hand, Inness' skies can be readily observed in New Jersey, the state in which he spent most of his mature years, just as Charles Burchfield's skies are best seen in his native Ohio and Thomas Hart Benton's skies appear only in Middle Western states like Missouri. But, since Inness believed that the final ends of all things lay in the Divine mind, he probably sought to capture in his landscapes not tangible objects but their earthly vibrations. He painted as if "there is such a thing as the indefinable which hides itself that we may feel after it." [12]

Intimate in scale and personal in nature, Inness' late paintings have a subjective response different from the earlier Hudson River School manner, and they also reveal a poetic streak that had been present in American art at least from the time of Washington Allston. The fact

7–19. GEORGE INNESS, *The Afterglow,* 1893.

7–20. GEORGE INNESS, *On the Delaware River*, 1873.

that Inness did survive and flourish in America indicates that both the country and its more reflective artists had learned how to tolerate each other and to create an environment open to further developments in the space of fifty years. A new art organization, the Society of American Artists, broke away from the now conservative National Academy of Design in 1877, and it encouraged personal expression in the arts. To a greater extent than before, patrons appeared who were willing to support the idiosyncratic development of particular artists. Certainly, painters lived in an artistic climate more favorable than that of Allston's generation and even than that in which the French Impressionists were forced to dwell. To be sure, painters like Inness did not re-evaluate so radically as the Impressionists the possibilities of form and color nor render their personal vision understandable only to initiates; moreover, the public still assumed that an artist's moral character directly affected the quality of his art and must reflect public morality and approximate the public's general sense of art appreciation. But if Inness could say that the purpose of a work of art was to awaken an emotion in the viewer akin to one in the artist rather than to appeal to the intellect or to instruct, American art had traveled far in a relatively short period of time.

CHAPTER EIGHT

The End of the Century

In the decades following the Civil War, the threads that had bound American art into a coherent pattern became unraveled as the realism of the Hudson River School and its various offshoots lost its hold on painters. European art, always a strong force in the minds of American artists, assumed greater relevance than it had prior to the War. At the Centennial Exposition of 1876, in Philadelphia, the comparison between the European and American exhibitions clarified in the minds of most viewers the poverty of American art. (The decisive competition between those favoring the nurture of a native art and those finding hope for an American painting only in the adaptation of European styles did not resolve itself until World War II, when those in the forefront of American art simply absorbed what they found useful in European avant-garde styles, particularly Surrealism, and channeled it in the directions appropriate to their own interests. In the period after the century's turn, Robert Henri and Alfred Stieglitz became part of and contributed to the polarization of attitude, and a large portion of the painting produced in the 1930's may be seen as the last major gathering of the forces favoring a strictly native development.)

Expatriation, an alternative taken by American artists since the days of Benjamin West, became a prominent feature of the American art scene, attracting such talents as James A. McNeill Whistler, Mary Cassatt, and John Singer Sargent. The most original of the expatriates, Whistler spent part of his youth in Russia (1843–48) and his young manhood in Paris (1855–59) before settling in London. Initially attracted to Gustave Courbet's realism, he subsequently modified his approach to form and subject matter partially under the influence of Japanese prints, preferring to emphasize flattened contours and abstract shapes through muted colors rather than create strong images by means of vigorous impasto (*Ill. 8–1*). Espousing the then radical notion that

8-1. JAMES A. MCNEILL WHISTLER, *Purple and Rose: The Lange Lijzen of the Six Marks,* 1864.

8–2. FRANK DUVENECK, *Old Town Brook, Polling, Bavaria, ca.* 1878.

form and color should exist for themselves alone, apart from subject, he called his works "nocturnes" and "symphonies" and stressed the decorative rather than the descriptive possibilities of painting.

The painters who returned to America from European study brought back a bewildering variety of styles, ranging from conservative academic and the poetic Barbizon modes, to the slashing brushstrokes of the Munich School (*Ill. 8–2*) and the color analyses of the Impressionists.

As American artists were picking through and combining various European styles in the years after the Civil War, so they also explored a wider variety of themes.

Men like John La Farge, Elihu Vedder, and Albert Pinkham Ryder worked with religious and Classical themes as well as with imagery evolved from the recesses of their own minds. Others, like Winslow Homer and Thomas Eakins, remained at home both physically and spiritually. Still others, like William Harnett and John F. Peto, narrowed the scope of art to the cataloging of objects, a recurrent preoccupation of American artists. Of the two, Harnett was the more disciplined, exhibiting a wider interest in varieties of objects and their textures. Peto, who worked within a more loosely conceived structural system, manipulated color more freely (*Ills. 8–3 and 8–4*). Harnett's work is the more tactile; Peto's emphasizes pictorial qualities.

From this period in which no single overriding attitude or artistic personality dominated the consciousness of artists and public, there emerged two of the very best painters in America's history, Homer and Eakins. The perplexing artistic situation can be viewed as a kind of metaphor for the fantastic changes then occurring in American life. As a result of rapid technological developments and industrial growth, coupled with the increasing philosophical conflict between science and religion, many basic human assumptions of an ideological, social, and religious nature were undermined and washed away. An urban culture began to replace the older rural one. Wealth, and with it, corruption, proliferated. It is no wonder that artists fled to Europe and escaped spiritually into the inward-turning world of art. And no wonder that those artists, particularly Homer, Eakins, and Ryder, who remained to observe the changes grew perplexed and have left us a body of work that records the confusion and intellectual disillusionments of the era.

Of the three, one (Ryder) was an eccentric and one (Homer) lived for many years as a recluse. None took part in the fundamental reexamination of color, line, and shape then convulsing French art, though Homer was somewhat affected by it. None achieved wide recognition in his lifetime or founded a school that carried on his style or point of view. Homer lived in New England, Ryder in New York, and Eakins in Philadelphia.

In his painting, Ryder moved along the path indicated by Inness' mystical landscapes, landscapes that were evocative of his moods and imaginative fancies. The private musings that Inness embodied in his trees and hazy suns, Ryder projected into the sea, just as similarly inclined twentieth-century artists like Darrel Austin and Morris Graves would incorporate their reflections into their paintings of animals and birds.

The sources of Ryder's art have never been fathomed. However, after he came to New York City from his native New Bedford, Massachusetts, in the late 1860's, he became a founder of the Society of

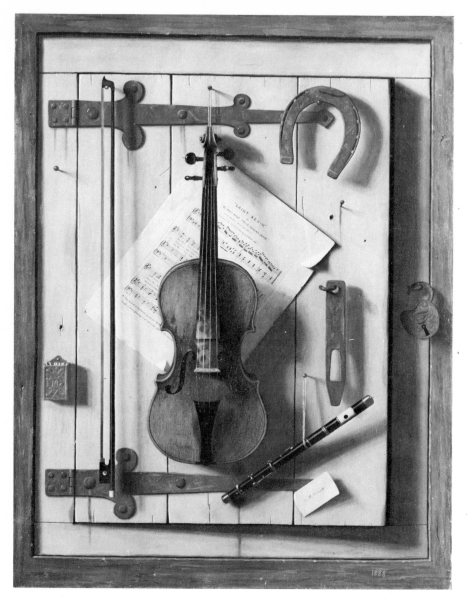

8–3. WILLIAM HARNETT, *Music and Good Luck,* 1888.

154

8–4. JOHN F. PETO, *Old Time Letter Rack*, 1894.

American Artists and may well have come to know intimately the paintings of Inness, Ralph Blakelock, and George Fuller, all of whom took a similar stylistic direction. But Ryder, more than the others, obscured the details that could tie a picture too closely to reality. He feared becoming a slave to detail and felt that an artist "should strive to express his thought and not the surface of it."[1] Once, early in his career, after he had grappled with the intricacies of objective observation, he related that he had come upon a scene framed in an opening between two trees. "It stood out like a painted canvas—the deep blue of a midday sky—a solitary tree brilliant with the green of early summer, a foundation of brown earth and gnarled roots. There was no detail to vex the eye. Three solid masses of form and color—sky, foliage and earth."[2] Ryder then reported that he laid on color with his palette knife. As his painting emerged on the canvas, he felt that it was better than nature because it was a new creation rather than a transcription. This attitude remained with him throughout his career.

The shapes he painted were almost invariably large in scale, and his attitude, even when his themes were derived from literature, was always personal. His color schemes are altogether unrelated to any sort of natural atmospheric effect. To achieve the impressions he sought, he built up thick textures with layers of underpainting, pigment, and glazes. Unfortunately, his paintings have aged so poorly that we can tell little more than that he usually opposed a range of yellows against one of blues or browns.

His sea and landscape paintings generally suggest the eternal rhythms of nature. The elements neither compete nor struggle with each other, nor is there any palpable sense of heroism or despair. Rather, a continuing rhythm is maintained by the artist to the point where it seems to tap a vast circuit of universal harmony. It is surprising, therefore, to realize that many of Ryder's literary paintings, which became a major part of his *oeuvre* after 1880, show violence and great activity. True, he often based these works on passages from Romantic authors like Coleridge that would lend themselves to such treatment,[3] but the serenity of *Toilers of the Sea* or *Moonlit Cove* (*Ills. 8–5 and 8–6*) hardly suggest that the passions of *Jonah* (*Ill. 8–7*) or *The Flying Dutchman* (in which we seem to be peering into chaos itself) are the products of one artistic temperament. Ryder frequently worked and reworked can-

8–5. ALBERT PINKHAM RYDER, *Toilers of the Sea,* before 1884.

8–6. ALBERT PINKHAM RYDER, *Moonlit Cove, ca.* 1890–1900.

vases over a period of years so that it is impossible to discern a chronological pattern in this strange discontinuity between his imaginative and his literary paintings. Whatever interior visions Ryder was subject to, they were not consistent with any rational scheme of development.

Just as one can enjoy the vagaries of Ryder's mind, so one can take pleasure in following the logical development of Winslow Homer's thought. His achievement, sustained over a half-century period, has never been equaled in the history of American art. Certainly one of the country's most profound artists, Homer probed the irreducibly basic elements of life disclosed in the contest for supremacy and survival.

His approach was typically American in that he eschewed philosophical theory and did not examine the mechanics of line, shape, and color as did his French contemporaries. He was not a form-giver nor a creator of new systems of visual thought. Rather, he sought to come to terms with life by observing life. A silent witness to the contest of forces loose in the world, the artist within him never replaced his essential humanity. In his work, particularly his later work, there is no picturesque sentiment, no moral uplift, no cold, polished surface or theatrical color. His canvases dispassionately reflect the unfinished, raw America of his day and convey the harsh problems of survival in that land.

Born in Boston and trained there as a lithographer, Homer came to New York City in 1859 and in the next few years gained renown for his magazine illustrations of the Civil War. He learned to observe and record essentials as well as to show movement economically, and he used variations of light and dark less for effect than for the sake of clarity. His early paintings reflect his training, and they indicate that light rather than character would be the chief vehicle for conveying his impressions. Generally, he would block out the main masses of his painting and instead of showing all the details in a crystal light, he would reveal the effect of light on those masses (*Ill. 8–8*). In contrast to Hudson River School work, his paintings concentrate on large forms in the landscape. Nor did he build up forms with a studio-dictated chiaroscuro to suggest roundness and bulk as Eastman John-

8–7. ALBERT PINKHAM RYDER, *Jonah, ca.* 1890.

son did *(see Ill. 7–16).* Homer understood that abrupt changes of light and dark approximate visual truth more nearly.

Throughout his life, Homer was especially interested in the effects of color, even waiting for days, as he once related, to observe a certain sea light. Approximating an Impressionist point of view he said that he recognized the differing effects of sky light, sunlight, and reflected light.[4] But he was not a true Impressionist, for his observations in paintings like *Long Branch* are frequently more accurate than theirs. He clearly understood the color-blurring rather than color-enhancing qualities of sunlight and the fact that, in strong sunlight, shadows are not perceived as different colors but as darker values, albeit lightly touched by a variety of colors.

8–8. WINSLOW HOMER, *Long Branch, New Jersey,* 1869.

Homer's vision, ultimately, was tonal rather than coloristic and based on careful observation of lighting effects in the northeastern part of the United States. However, within and in spite of those limitations, his work possesses a painterly breadth that the work of contemporaries lacks. Homer's ability to handle pattern more broadly and abstractly was also unique. Together, these features give his work its singular character. To some extent they may reflect the works of Manet and the examples of Japanese art he undoubtedly saw at the Universal Exposition, when he visited Paris in 1867.

Many of his paintings of this period are of young ladies at play or enjoying themselves at leisure. In these vacation pictures, Homer replaced the sentimentality of his contemporaries with a curious impersonality. His figures, unaware of the viewer's presence, do not act in genre scenes. They simply appear. In the eyes of one observer, Henry James, these works contained neither literature, imagination, refinement, nor selection.[5] Homer's paintings seemed hopelessly unfinished.

During the 1870's his paintings remained as "unfinished" as before, but his palette darkened and his mood shifted. He seemed to recognize that neither moral force, altruistic force, nor individual strength of character affected life as much as the natural forces that operated competitively. In the paintings of his maturity, man was increasingly opposed to nature. Homer portrayed huntsmen, not sportsmen (*Ill. 8–9*). The watercolor studies he made during trips to the Bahamas in 1885 and 1899 often showed the islanders in dangerous situations as they searched for food (*Ill. 8–10*). Following a visit to England in 1881, he tended to substitute fishermen for huntsmen until, finally, he let the land, sea, and sky contend with each other, heedless of the existence of man (*see Ill. 8–15*). In this sense, he painted neither views nor panoramas, but the hostile solitude where forces were in constant competition with each other. If Thomas Cole dimly felt and expressed this in a literary way, Homer penetrated its actuality, expressing it in terms of physical sensation rather than emotional postures.

In works like *Two Guides*, Homer's modifications of the Hudson River School style are apparent. Individual leaves and flowers are recorded in floating brushstrokes. The textures that distinguish plant life

8–9. WINSLOW HOMER, *Two Guides*, 1876.

8–10. WINSLOW HOMER, *After the Hurricane, Bahamas, ca.* 1898–99.

8–11. WINSLOW HOMER, *The Fog Warning,* 1885.

8–12. WINSLOW HOMER, *Hunter in the Adirondacks*, 1892.

and cloud forms are emphasized. Suppression of detail causes landscape features to merge in broad, extended planes. Although changes in value appear as darkened shadows and brightened highlights, which help locate forms in space, a greater colorism than characterizes Hudson River School painting is also present. But most important, human figures rise from Homer's landscape, rather than disappear into it. They do not act in sympathy with a benign nature. With ax or gun in hand, or pulling on oars, Homer's figures confront the landscape, each seeking in it his means of survival.

In his seascapes of the Maine coast done after 1883, he reveals great respect for the sea itself, endowing it with a real solidity. It reflects the cold Maine skies but it is not transparent. Generating colors, textures, and densities as well as emotions of its own, it becomes—unlike Ryder's and Eakins' seas—a protagonist in an endless drama (*Ill. 8–11, and see Ills. 8–5 and 8–18*).

Homer's ability to convey weather conditions and the physical feeling of particular landscapes without subordinating nature's solid substance to its surface appearance is one of the hallmarks of his style. Even in his watercolors, this characteristic is apparent, whether in his earlier studies, in those of the late 1880's, or even later when he pioneered the use of calligraphic strokes and a technique of overrunning and smearing edges (*Ill. 8–12*). Unlike his exact contemporary Cézanne, who was concerned with problems of surface and color organization, of interlocking shapes, of relating near and distant forms, of suggesting the interchangeability of foreground and background shapes (*Ill. 8–13*), Homer strove to project a sense of the forest itself, its menace, its spaces, its shafts of light, its stillness, and the freshness of its air. Homer painted from life, Cézanne from a conception of art.

After 1890 Homer staged his dramas often without the participation of human beings. *The Fox Hunt* portrays, with the flattened space and broad planes of a Japanese print, a battle for life; *Northeaster* goes beyond the struggle for existence to the opposition of elemental forces (*Ills. 8–14 and 8–15*). One wonders, therefore, if *The Gulf Stream* (*Ill. 8–16*) is not, in effect, a portrait of both the artist and his era—contending with life and elemental forces, but ultimately helpless before them. The hopelessness that Homer seems to project at the end of the century is in striking contrast to Cole's optimism at mid-century (*see Ill. 6–6*). Like other Americans in the 1890's and after, he, too, seems hesitant and confused.[6]

In a sense the increasingly solitary man was reliving (particularly in his late seascapes) the fundamental American experiences of the Atlantic crossing and confrontation with the "howling wilderness"; but he was also reflecting the consuming interest of the late nineteenth century in the principles of Darwinian evolution. These pervaded whole areas of thought, affecting basic attitudes toward institutions, religions, and science. (One contemporary historian considered even the Society of American Artists to be not so much a part of a movement of reform, as another stage in the progress of American art, "destined, when it has accomplished its end, to be in turn succeeded by yet higher steps in the scale of advance. . . ."[7]) While Homer's fellow New Englanders John Fiske and Henry Ward Beecher illustrated the ways in which man was happily thought to cap the entire evolutionary

8–13. PAUL CÉZANNE, *Pines and Rocks, ca.* 1904.

sequence,[8] Homer viewed the other side of the Darwinian scheme more closely—that dealing with the survival of the fittest.

In spite of his seclusion at Prout's Neck, Maine, Homer's preoccupations were similar to those of contemporary literary figures he may or may not have known. His paintings paralleled, in their images of violence, the Darwinian novels of Stephen Crane and Frank Norris. And one might also say that Homer responded to the Maine coast somewhat as Hamlin Garland to the Middle West—still acknowledging the raw beauty of the land, but recognizing it as a stark, amoral

8–14. WINSLOW HOMER, *The Fox Hunt*, 1893.

8–15. WINSLOW HOMER, *Northeaster*, 1895.

8–16. WINSLOW HOMER, *The Gulf Stream,* 1899.

entity, capable of killing as well as sustaining life. By asserting these aspects of landscape, Homer seems to be pronouncing the end of the American dream of the land as solace and source of spiritual sustenance. In Homer's paintings, the nineteenth century had indeed come to an end.

Homer gained a sizable reputation in his old age, but he was not lionized as were artists who, in their paintings of sentimental scenes or religious dramas, catered to a less demanding and less stringent public taste. Thomas Eakins, with whom Homer shared a certain similarity of outlook, enjoyed even less public recognition during his lifetime. And both, although their fame increased considerably in the years following their deaths, like earlier colonial artists would have only the most minimal influence on succeeding generations.

Eakins was born, lived, and died in Philadelphia, and he taught there, at the Pennsylvania Academy of the Fine Arts, from 1876 to 1886. Yet, his was not an urban art nor did he concentrate upon the city in which so much of his painting was done. Instead, and particularly after 1880, when he largely abandoned landscape and genre for portraiture, Eakins' art transcended place and became the embodiment of a state of mind then prevalent in American society, one of disillusionment and frustration, even of despair. Both he and his subjects seem to have realized that they were the last, that after them neither the urbane nor the intelligent would serve as subjects for art because they had become irrelevant in an industrial, mechanized, and commercial world.

Eakins' profound realizations of character grew from an initial impersonal and realistic vision not unlike Homer's. Eakins studied art in Paris between 1866 and 1870 under Jean-Léon Gérôme, an academician of the École des Beaux-Arts. From his master, he absorbed steady discipline and a desire to create an honest, straightforward art. "I hate affectation," he wrote to his parents during his student days. Like Charles Willson Peale, but quite unlike Samuel F. B. Morse, whose grandiose misunderstanding of his own abilities helped annul his slender talents, Eakins was to say, "I think I can make my name as a painter, for I am learning to make solid heavy work." [9]

Like Copley's American works, Eakins' paintings are matter-of-fact. He dissected cadavers and used a primitive type of moving-picture camera to better understand human movement. Determined to place his forms with absolute precision in space, he studied perspective with extreme diligence, as his sketches reveal. "All the sciences are done in a simple way," he once said. "In mathematics the complicated things are reduced to simple things. So it is in painting." [10] Although Eakins could draw on his professional training, he was (like, say, Ralph Earl) still more concerned with ways of looking at things than with theories about representing things.

Evidently, Eakins' vision was even less disturbed than Homer's by Japanese prints or Manet's paintings, which he, too, might have seen in Paris at the Exposition in 1867. In his genre pieces of the 1870's, his desire to subordinate pattern and light and atmosphere to the realization of form is evident, even in outdoor scenes (*Ill. 8–17*). For him, sunlight did not dissolve objects, but emphasized their solidity. There is no drama in these works nor even an anecdotal quality to flavor them. Instead, there is a precision and clarity, in the distant forms as well as the near, that bespeaks Eakins' intent to record rather than interpret. This quality is easily noted when comparing boating scenes

8–17. THOMAS EAKINS, *Max Schmitt in a Single Scull*, 1871.

by Eakins and Homer in which the basic forms are similarly placed (*Ill. 8–18, and see Ill. 8–11*).

Eakins' sober analyses were enlivened by an unobtrusive imaginativeness that gave his paintings a force far beyond that of mere documentation. The masterpiece of his early years, and perhaps of his career, *The Gross Clinic* (*Ill. 8–19*), is a portrait of both a man and his work, a type of portrait seen earlier in American art, but carried much further (*see Ill. 5–17*). The dominant form of Dr. Gross, illuminated by a Rembrandtesque light, mediates compositionally and intellectually between the detachment of the students and the active involvement of the doctors.[11] Dr. Gross's bloody hand, a sensational bit of reporting, underlines both the routine nature of the operation as well as its quickened life-and-death aspects: He is both a heroic figure, and a man engaged in his ordinary work. An objective study, it is nevertheless warm and passionate, and Eakins' appreciation of Gross's human and professional qualities is apparent.

Because of his ability to realize the nature of human character, Eakins proved to be the country's finest portrait painter. To be sure,

8–18. THOMAS EAKINS, *Starting Out After Rail*, 1874.

8–19. THOMAS EAKINS, *The Gross Clinic*, 1875.

he usually painted people whose intelligence had earned his friendship and whose personalities were familiar to him so that he was able to bring out distinctive aspects of their character. But what might have become in less capable and less understanding hands a series of standardized portraits became instead analyses of both a class and a group of highly individual persons. *The Thinker* (*Ill. 8-20*) both in name and conception might be considered the leitmotiv of Eakins' portraits, which include some of the most beautiful and individual faces ever realized in American art (*Ill. 8-21*).

8–20. THOMAS EAKINS, *The Thinker:*
Louis N. Kenton, 1900.

8–21. THOMAS EAKINS, *Addie,* 1900.

172

8–22. THOMAS EAKINS, *The Swimming Hole*, 1883.

In the relatively few genre scenes that Eakins painted after 1885, a hushed silence substitutes for profundity. This sense of stillness was emphasized by the restrictive compositional formulas which he imposed either in the form of triangles, as in *The Swimming Hole* (*Ill. 8–22*), or a grid of horizontals and verticals, as in *Between Rounds* (*Ill. 8–23*). These nude and semi-nude studies are among the few he ever attempted because he preferred to paint the undraped body engaged in an activity appropriate to nudity. Such logic informed all of Eakins' work. Its realism was tempered by reflection. In a wildly boisterous age, he painted some of the "quietest" works in American art. Their spirit was, in the first years of the new century, challenged by an art closer in mood to the quickening tempo of life that left Eakins and his generation behind.

8–23. THOMAS EAKINS, *Between Rounds,* 1899.

CHAPTER NINE

Early Twentieth-Century Realism

Had Eakins and Homer spent their last years in New York or even in sections of the Middle and Far West, they would have witnessed a refurbishing of the American spirit, whose disillusion and pessimism their paintings so bleakly described. In many urban and rural centers, a broad-scale revitalization of American life had begun, and an era of reform known as the Progressive Movement ensued. In government, business, labor, and education, profound changes were occurring. Rooted in the need to understand the realities of life in the modern era, an increasing social awareness helped create a climate of opinion favorable to eliminating grosser aspects of American life. The America that was once considered an extended Genesis now had to be reconstituted lest it become an extended hell.

But most artists (not just Eakins and Homer) ignored the changes then taking place. A visit to practically any exhibition or studio around 1900 would have revealed little awareness or appreciation of the intellectual and social ferment that was vitalizing Middle Western Populists and urban muckrakers. Artists were still painting in a variety of styles ranging from neoclassicism to a watered-down Barbizon impressionism, and subject matter ranged from the gentle to the genteel.

Although a few strikingly original artists such as Eakins and Homer were at work in the last decades of the nineteenth century, there had developed no really rebellious alternative to this conservatism. No radical groups created traditions of their own or established alternative histories of art. But partially in response to a desire to cut through the artificialities of conservative taste and to understand better the effects of increasing urbanization, some artists began turning to themes of city life. They often found their subject matter in the endless events and non-events that fill the days of city dwellers. Other artists, although undoubtedly aware of the impress of the city on their consciousness, found justification for their art within art itself, turning painting into the primary instrument of their sensibilities rather than using it as an instrument to record visual data. These artists, enamored of Parisian modernism, gravitated toward the life and style of that city, continuing, in effect, the old dependence upon a European center for artistic direction.

These two groups sometimes existed in friendly rivalry, but they were both unalterably opposed by the still strongly entrenched forces of conservatism. In effect, a twin-pronged avant-garde came into being early in the new century, the one exploring subject matter foreign to old-fashioned ideals of beauty, uplift, and goodness, the other leaving behind traditional attitudes toward pictorial form, color, and realization of subject matter.

Two exhibitions symbolically mark the triumph of these progressive tendencies, that of The Eight in 1908 and the Armory Show in 1913. The earlier exhibition, composed predominantly of realistic paintings by Robert Henri—the leader of the group—John Sloan, George Luks, Everett Shinn, and William Glackens, also included works by the Impressionist Ernest Lawson, the painter of fantasy Arthur B. Davies, and the Post-Impressionist Maurice Prendergast. The Armory Show introduced modern art to America on a large scale. Although subsequently overrated, both exhibitions have an important function in the history of American art. To a still perpetually embarrassed American art audience, they serve as American equivalents of the famous nineteenth- and twentieth-century European exhibitions of modern art— indications of American artistic relevance and vitality in the early twentieth century as well as apologies for the fact that America did not produce a Picasso or a Matisse to help change the course of art. In point of fact, the realists among The Eight, in one combination or another, had exhibited together since 1901, and most American modernists had gone abroad before the Armory Show opened in 1913. These two exhibitions are, therefore, of greater importance to the history of taste and of criticism than of art.

Artists like Jerome Myers had been painting the poor people of New York City since the 1890's, but it was the group of artists around Robert Henri that assumed the dominant role in the new realism. They recorded aspects of the lives of the wealthy as well as the poor, some of the turbulence of the big city and its landscape, and that quality of gusto in American life symbolized by Theodore Roosevelt. They seem to have been most closely in accord from about 1900 to 1910, when each began increasingly to develop his own personality and interests.

The leader of the realists, Cincinnati-born Robert Henri, was, paradoxically, not the best painter of the group, but he was an effective teacher and spokesman. Through his encouragement, Sloan, Luks, Shinn, and Glackens, whom he had met in Philadelphia, began to paint seriously. Their friendship continued after they left that city, one by one, for New York between 1896 and 1904.

They went out into the streets as earlier artists had gone into the countryside to paint what they might find, trying to capture both the random gestures and the underlying truths in the lives of the people they met. "Art cannot be separated from life," Henri often reminded them.[1] Enamored of life, they wanted to make art from life. For them, as for Tolstoy, whose writings influenced them considerably, art was an activity by which one person transmitted his feelings to another. "Draw a man so that you *show* what he is," George Luks once said.[2]

Their celebrations of life were random ones. They were less concerned with social betterment than with conveying their excitement at simply being alive. As trained newspaper illustrators (with the exception of Henri), they refrained from over-editorializing. They did not necessarily search out particular types and scenes to paint nor work out their personal obsessions. Instead, they produced a sampling of images observed in rambles through the city and, often after 1910, through the countryside. Art was a sidewalk spectacle, and the poor—when they did paint the poor—became a new kind of noble savage. In fact, Glackens and Myers both said that there was in the slums a joy of living not found elsewhere, a purity of being more conventional (wealthy) people could ill afford[3]—an opinion corroborated in the paintings of all the realists.

Although Luks' famous remark "Art—my slats! Guts! Guts! Life! Life! I can paint with a shoestring dipped in pitch and lard" is very like Frank Norris' "Who cares for fine style! Tell your yarn and let your style go to the devil. We don't want literature, we want life,"[4] the Henri circle had less in common with contemporary novelists and muckracking journalists than one might imagine. Their art had little of the hard realism or gritty determinism that characterizes the works of Norris, Stephen Crane, Theodore Dreiser, Lincoln Steffens, and Upton Sinclair, even though their subject matter was often drawn from the same sources. They preferred to communicate an immediacy of mood and a heightened response. Concerned with capturing the gestures and features of their subjects as well as expressing their own feelings in the presence of their subjects, they eschewed larger meanings implicit in them.

The more easily to convey their excitement, they adopted sketchlike techniques, in which brushstrokes acted as conductors of emotion. "The brushstroke, at the moment of contact, carries inevitably the exact state of being of the artist at that exact moment into the world," Henri said.[5] No wonder he sought out earlier artists whose brushwork seemed quick and fast—artists like Hals, Velázquez, the early Manet, and Henri's fellow Cincinnatian Frank Duveneck (see Ill. 8–2), and introduced their craft to his friends.

But for all their similarities, they were different as men and as artists. Henri, the oldest, approached subject matter in the most traditional way. Many of his studies of New York are quiet scenes from which he held himself at a certain distance (Ills. 9–1 and 9–2). His notations are quick and summary, but despite his insistence on spontaneity and directness and his desire to give his immediate impressions through his brushwork, a Whistlerian stillness pervades his work. It would seem that the main thrust of his philosophy was carried by his portraits. To these, he applied a dynamism that equaled the intensity of his words (Ill. 9–3). In them, he could mirror best his own emotions. "I am looking at each individual with the eager hope of finding something of the dignity of life, the humor, the humanity, the kindness."[6] Painted directly with no preliminary drawing or concern for outdoor lighting, these portraits convey Henri's momentary exaltations. Although he was a student of Eakins' pupil Thomas Anshutz at the Pennsylvania Academy of the Fine Arts, no two artists seem to be further apart in technique and attitude than Eakins and Henri.

George Luks' brushmanship was even looser than Henri's. He projected a lusty image of himself and, like his friends, his intelligence was informed primarily by his feelings. Though in his work bragga-

9–1. ROBERT HENRI, *The East River, New York, ca.* 1900–1905.

9–2. ROBERT HENRI, *West 57th Street, New York,* 1902.

docio often substituted for basic talent, he could muster occasional insights such as inspirit his portrayal of the faded glories of *The Old Duchess* (*Ill. 9–4*), but he usually mined a sentimental vein close to that of his more traditional contemporaries. His slum children are urbanized Spanish or Italian peasants, picturesque as can be (*Ill. 9–5*).

Luks saw himself as a kind of superman; however, it remained for the slightly younger George Bellows to say, "The ideal artist is he who knows everything, feels everything, experiences everything, and retains his experience in a spirit of wonder and feeds upon it with creative lust. . . . The ideal artist is the superman."[7] Bellows, who became a pupil of Henri soon after he arrived in New York in 1904 from his native Ohio (but who did not join The Eight in their 1908 exhibition), caught most completely the dynamic qualities of modern life. His scale was vaster than that of his friends. Man was the primary unit of study for them, and Bellows often multiplied him into a crowd (*Ill. 9–6, and see Ill. 9–12*). Not content with painting urban vignettes, he tried to symbolize in his art the energies that seemed to pulse through the city.

9-4. GEORGE LUKS, *The Old Duchess*, 1905.

9–5. GEORGE LUKS, *The Spielers,* 1905.

9–6. GEORGE BELLOWS, *Cliff Dwellers,* 1913.

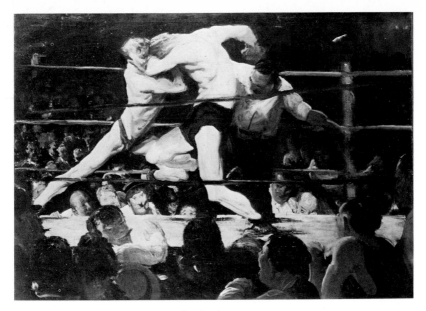

9–7. GEORGE BELLOWS, *Stag at Sharkey's,* 1907.

9–8. GEORGE BELLOWS, *The Lone Tenement,* 1909.

Yet, like those of his contemporaries, his paintings do not have the aura of dramatic conflict that one finds in Homer's work. Bellows' paintings are carried along on a stream of physical energy. His many prizefight pictures reduce to the level of entertainment the forces of opposition that Homer had employed to express the essential dramas of existence (*Ill. 9–7*). *The Lone Tenement* (*Ill. 9–8*) is a poignant documentation of urban renewal rather than a battleground of old and new, rich and poor—whatever are the urban equivalents of sea and land, life and death. Bellows and other realists could paint what they saw and felt, but not what must be grasped by the imagination. *Men of the Docks* (*Ill. 9–9*), the confrontation of a large ocean liner with tall buildings and strong horses, remains a mordant observation of life on the docks, and only suggests what forces these elements represent. Yet, only Bellows juxtaposed so many images of strength and energy that symbolized the tensions and creative forces of the modern city (*see Ills. 9–1 and 9–15*).

His sense of form was also the best developed, whether in establishing loosely organized triangular or circular patterns or in opposing large planes to hold his paintings together (*see Ills. 9–6 and 9–9*). Within these large units, he often let the light and dark tones create linked patterns that tie his forms more cohesively to each other. Invariably, he imposed a kind of grid on his picture surfaces, but, like most American painters, he did not integrate all the forms on the grid. While a contemporary European artist like Picasso, more concerned with the entire field of the canvas than individual components, would maintain a flux and an easy give-and-take between objects and the surrounding field, Bellows rarely assimilated object and field. His *Polo at Lakewood* (*Ill. 9–10*), for example, although ultimately based on racecourse paintings of Manet and Degas, reveals a totally different conception of art than that of the Europeans. Bellows clearly detaches his figures from the background instead of making them part of the tapestry of the whole. The clouds in the sky are related to the polo players and the observers by means of tones and colors, but not in terms of configurations of shape.

Since Bellows' sense of form was better developed than that of his fellow realists, it is not surprising that he would seek a more precise

9–9. GEORGE BELLOWS, *Men of the Docks*, 1912.

9–10. GEORGE BELLOWS, *Polo at Lakewood*, 1910.

way to organize his canvases after seeing the modern European paintings at the Armory Show. Around 1917 he learned of Jay Hambidge's theory of Dynamic Symmetry, a mathematical system governing the relationships of geometrical units within a work of art. Its effect on Bellows was to rigidify rather than to tighten his sense of structure and, curiously, to force him to explore traditional methods of chiaroscuro modeling (*Ill. 9–11, and see Ill. 9–7*). The primary result of his studies was an increased separation between object and field as well as a lessening in immediacy of mood and presence, the *sine qua non* of the realists.

Similar problems troubled John Sloan when he began in his later works to use pictorial rather than storytelling motifs. In his early years, and frequently later, he maintained that art was the response of the living to life, and that life was the primary motif of art. "Work which is purely non-representational loses some of the texture of life," he said,[8] and this attitude remains the key to his painting.

9–11. GEORGE BELLOWS, *Dempsey and Firpo,* 1924.

9–12. JOHN SLOAN, *Woman's Work*, ca. 1911.

The last of The Eight to leave Philadelphia, Sloan moved to New York in 1904, where he soon became the most tireless recorder of city life. He catalogued its trivia with the eyes of an anonymous city dweller, painting views of life in apartments seen across the courtyard, in yards and streets, and down the block. In his work the city became a place of nondirected sensation interpreted with little sentimentality or grandiosity, lacking even anecdotal moments that would provide the-

matic richness. Images of people bathing, cooking, washing, and walk-
ing are given without the frequent posturizing of Luks or Bellows.
They are there to be seen and savored for whatever qualities they offer.
Of The Eight, Sloan was the quintessential realist, never questioning,
hardly modifying, always recording (*Ills. 9–12, 9–13, and 9–14*).

By what must have been a strong act of will, Sloan was able to assume the undiscriminating eye of a camera when, in fact, he was a
man of strong opinion. To evoke the proper atmosphere for a picture,
he found it necessary for the artist "to go among *common people*—not
to waste his time among his fellows, for it must be from the other
class . . . that he will get his knowledge of life." [9] So infatuated was he
with human life that he even refused to consider the relationship between art and the machine. Art had no mission to interpret the modern Machine Age, he believed, and he seriously questioned the importance of a Machine Age itself as a twentieth-century phenomenon.[10]
He even tried to keep his political interests separate from his painting.
The most politically motivated of The Eight, he provided illustrations
for *The Masses* from 1912 to 1916 and for other left-wing journals
afterward. But the socialistic attitudes that informed his political work
affected his painting in only the most general terms. He never painted
tracts, only people.

In his earliest work, the palette is relatively dark and monochro-
matic, enlivened only by occasional touches of color. But these he
dabbed on in quick touches that conveyed through their rough finish a
sense of liveness (*Ill. 9–16*). His abrupt juxtaposition of darks and
lights enhance the feeling of movement. After 1928, Sloan experimented with brighter colors in order to model forms strongly and
build them up with layers of glaze and underpaint. Like Bellows'
paintings of the 1920's, Sloan's later work is often volumetric and
static.

William Glackens had no such trouble with color, revealing as early
as 1905 a freedom of touch and tone surprising in one trained as a
newspaper illustrator. In both his use of color and his brushstroke,
Glackens' affinities were with French Impressionism, particularly with
Renoir, whose works he might have seen when abroad in 1895. So, too,
was his attitude to subject matter, and he soon became a painter of
festive scenes, of people enjoying themselves at the theater or prome-

9–13. JOHN SLOAN, *Little Movie Theater*, 1913.

9–14. JOHN SLOAN, *The White Way*, 1926.

nading in the park, or bathing (*Ill. 9–15, and see Ills. 9–18 and 9–19*). He was little disturbed by life's struggles or the burdens of urban existence.

Despite his experimentation with Impressionist techniques, Glackens' work retained a distinctive American quality. It is obvious in the prudery of his *Nude with Apple* (*Ill. 9–17*), a type of subject few Americans have been able to handle easily (in this century one thinks of artists like Leon Kroll, who placed his reclining Venus on a hillside but in a bathrobe, and the Pop artist Tom Wesselmann who turned his into a plastic doll).

American, too (though less obtrusive), is Glackens' insistence on defining objects, letting them maintain their integrity within the overall scheme. Glackens pumped air and depth into his *The Drive, Central Park* (*Ill. 9–18*), giving objects a space of their own, while Maurice Prendergast, the first American to understand the Post-Impressionist direction, had already learned to emphasize shapes that adhere to the picture surface (*see Ill. 10–2*). When Glackens is closest to Renoir, his

9–15. WILLIAM GLACKENS, *View of the East River from Brooklyn*, 1902.

9–16. JOHN SLOAN, *Three A. M.,* 1909.

9–17. WILLIAM GLACKENS, *Nude with Apple,* 1910.

9–18. WILLIAM GLACKENS, *The Drive, Central Park, ca.* 1905.

9–19. WILLIAM GLACKENS, *Beach Scene, New London,* 1918.

figures never dissolve into atmosphere or vaguely defined areas of color, but stand out sharply and clearly (*Ill. 9–19*).

It would be easy, but incorrect, to conclude that Glackens misunderstood modern European art. His basic visualization of forms was, simply, different. But this difference informs the work of so many American painters, realist and abstractionist alike, that it implies a distinctly national visual set. An American would not have invented Cubism—not because of an artistic provincialism or a disinclination to engage in philosophical speculation—but because the American vision interprets each object for itself, not as part of an integrated field. In the early years of the twentieth century, American painters were still searching for objects, but now they were finding them in the city as well as in the countryside.

CHAPTER TEN

First-Generation Modernism

While the realists were wandering the streets of New York in search of subject matter, another group of artists was learning about the revolution taking place in the ateliers of Paris and other European cities. By 1913, when the Association of American Painters and Sculptors staged the Armory Show in New York, a number of painters had already received considerable education abroad. Probably not since the days of West and Copley had American artists been so aware of the latest developments in the art world. Some did contribute directly to the radical innovations then being made, but they lacked the sustained purpose and superb inventiveness of the European artists.

They were like children wanting to sample each piece of candy at the corner store, and they tasted voraciously: Fauvism, Cubism, Futurism, and the varieties of Expressionism. Some, like Arthur Dove and John Marin, managed to forge personal styles. Others, bewildered by the richness of choice, lost their sense of personal identity and imitated now one, now another, European painter. Still others, after initial forays into twentieth-century modernism, recoiled and either returned to realistic representation or went back to Cézanne's paintings for their lessons.

No single style emerged from this generation of American modernists. They did, however, share at least one important aim with their European counterparts. They wanted to penetrate the reality behind surface appearances, and they tapped the wealth of available styles and approaches to do it. The results of their probings were often translated to the canvas world by means of form, composition, color, and expressions of psychological states of being, and much of their work takes place, therefore, just on the far side of verbal explanation.

"Art dies when the natural dominates," Max Weber once said.[1] He and others made visual their spiritual searches in a recalcitrant material world. Animated by the belief that art should express ideas rather than things, they gave form to feelings by means of an abstract artistic language. They would have agreed with Ernest Fenollosa, the Orientalist and art educator whose influence had already been felt, when he wrote in 1906, "The self that we find is something far deeper than the froth of personality, something that belongs to all free spirits, as to nature." [2]

Why the interest in abstract art and in contemporary European movements? Why the desire to develop the extreme sensibility requisite for painting abstractly and plumbing the understructure of reality where, as Max Weber suggested, "Even thought is matter"? [3] Just as European artists were experiencing the crunch of modern civilization, so, too, were Americans. Artists both at home and abroad desired a basic reform of human life, not just the obvious social reforms that the muckrakers were seeking. At a time when the car and the airplane were becoming effective symbols of the increasing speed of living, and the sounds of industry were drowning out the single human voice, artists began to insist on the importance of contemplation, of individual emotional response, of reverie, and of the cultivation of the senses. As much as abstract art reflected advanced philosophical and physical concepts, it also reflected an overwhelming desire to humanize life once again and to allow the individual to participate in it on a level meaningful to him. For the circle around Alfred Stieglitz, the primary channel by which abstract art was introduced to America, the central preoccupation was with creating a new civilization, a new culture, and a new world. [4] Stieglitz, Max Weber, John Marin, Georgia O'Keeffe, among others, were like primitives of a new beginning.

The desire to participate in contemporary European movements was also symptomatic of the age. Increasing immigration had brought additional millions to the country, and, in New York, it helped create a literate and cultivated milieu. Moreover, men like Stieglitz, Weber, Abraham Walkowitz, and others who were perhaps not even a generation removed from Europe favored a broad internationalism that prompted quick and immediate appreciation of European cultural developments. Concurrently, international trade grew tremendously and foreign affairs became foreign involvement. Theodore Roosevelt's offer in 1905 to mediate between the principals in the Russo-Japanese War and Max Weber's efforts in 1907 to organize a class under Matisse have similar implications.

The first artist to understand Parisian modernism was not a member of the Stieglitz circle. From the mid-1890's Maurice Prendergast, who exhibited with The Eight, had been painting with a greater sense of responsibility to form and color than to theme and with a greater commitment to the expression of his feelings than to the recording of appearance. His city views of waterfront and park, unlike those of Henri, Bellows, Sloan, and Glackens, are neither mood pieces, attractive vignettes of city life, nor celebrations of urban dynamism. They are controlled exercises in brush technique, figure placement, and color relationship (*Ill. 10–1, and see Ills. 9–1, 9–9, and 9–15*).

Although Prendergast had lived in France between 1891 and 1895, it was only after his trip to Italy in the last two years of the century that he began to control depth relationships, a major aspect of the modernist technique. The bright colors and assertive brushwork in the middleground of Prendergast's works acknowledge his study of the French Nabis, including Bonnard and Vuillard (*Ill. 10–2*). But despite

10–1. MAURICE PRENDERGAST, *The East River*, 1901.

repeated trips abroad after 1900, Prendergast never passed beyond the Parisian styles of the 1890's, when the Nabi manner was developed. Despite an evident knowledge of Fauve painting and despite subtle changes in his own art, his work always retained a *fin de siècle* feeling. His subjects pass their time in Arcadian settings and they respond to them with the same uncomplicated joy that Prendergast seemingly possessed when he painted them.

It was Alfred Stieglitz, a photographer, who brought American painting into the twentieth century. At his various galleries (the Photo-Secession Gallery, later called 291 because of its Fifth Avenue address [1905–17], the Intimate Gallery [1925–29], and An American Place [1930–51],) Americans were introduced to the European modernists. Stieglitz proselytized for an American modernism and supported many American painters but developed special affinities with John Marin, Arthur Dove, and Georgia O'Keeffe, three artists who developed strong styles that were relatively independent of European movements. Their respect and admiration for Stieglitz were almost complete. When

10–2. MAURICE PRENDERGAST, *The Flying Horses,* 1908–9.

asked what Stieglitz meant to him as an artist, Dove said simply, "Everything." [5]

It was Max Weber, however, who probably understood Parisian modernism better than any of his contemporaries. And this was his artistic undoing. A man of passionate temperament, as his later paintings show, he steeped himself in various styles—now Fauvism, now Cubism, now Futurism—before he could finally paint the images he found within himself. The career of Arshile Gorky parallels that of Weber's to a certain degree, suggesting that one substratum of American art is inhabited by displaced cosmopolitans who find their own language only in their maturity.

The Russian-born Weber had received the most advanced art training available in America before sailing for France in 1905. Late in the previous decade, he studied with Arthur Dow, an admirer of Gauguin as well as a close friend and exponent of Ernest Fenollosa's doctrines. As early as 1894, Dow had realized that pictorial composition was "not merely an assemblage of objects truthfully represented," it was "the *expression of an idea,* and all the parts must be so related as to form a harmonious whole." [6] Through Dow's use of abstract patterns and oriental designs, Weber had learned to see forms in terms of visual relations rather than as discrete objects years before he traveled abroad.

His *Chinese Restaurant (Ill. 10-4)* is a kind of *summa* of styles and influences available to a receptive artist around 1915. The bright, unmodeled colors of Fauve painting and American Indian art (Weber had also carefully observed Kachina dolls and other primitive artifacts) intensify an essentially Synthetic Cubist painting. Forms suggesting differing textural surfaces overlap as in a collage, and the repetitive film-sequence images of Futurism give added life to the forms in the center. Yet, like most of Weber's paintings, it is not purely a formal exercise, but has an expressive content. Of this painting, he wrote that contrasts between the dark night and the "maze and blaze of light" inside the restaurant split its interior into fragments; this and the color and movement could only be captured by "kaleidoscopic means." [7] The work, then, is an emotional visualization with modern techniques.

In other works, Weber became more primitive, more Cézannesque, and more Cubist by turns. In the 1920's, his forms approximated Picasso's "neoclassic" style. From the 1920's through the 1940's, Weber's ex-

10–3. MAX WEBER, *Adoration of the Moon*, 1944.

pressionistic tendencies would break through the Cubist reserve. He often painted scenes of orthodox Jewish life, a kind of subject matter that suited his changing style, especially that alluding to the mystical experiences of the ultra-strict Hasidic sect. In these paintings, the interrupted planes, odd coloration, transparent passages, and unstable gravity are a visual embodiment of the intense religiosity of these people with whom Weber often identified (*Ill. 10–3*).

In the years before World War I, when the implications of Post-Impressionist styles and theories were being explored in Cubism, Fauvism, and other movements, two American artists believed that their work, which they called Synchromism, made a novel contribution. They issued manifestos when in Europe (the first Americans to do so) and exhibited in Munich and Paris in 1913. Much to their dismay, they were dismissed as followers of the Europeans who were known as Orphists.

The Synchromism of Stanton Macdonald-Wright and Morgan Russell was based, like Orphism, on the Neo-Impressionism of Seurat and Signac as well as the scientific and theoretical sources the older artists

10–4. MAX WEBER, *Chinese Restaurant*, 1915.

had used, including such studies as Michel Eugène Chevreul's *De la loi du contraste simultané des couleurs* (1839) and Ogden Rood's *Modern Chromatics* (1879). Color became the chief generative agent in their paintings, and it was used to suggest spatial advances and recessions. Although natural objects were largely eliminated, Russell found in the movement of light and color a metaphor for the universal movement of life, and Macdonald-Wright saw in them a metaphor for the rhythms of human anatomy.[8] Never before had American artists given up so completely their concentration on recognizable objects. Their art shows a desire to come abreast of European developments, if not take the lead away from European artists.

Basic to their work was an understanding of the form-building possibilities of the flattened plane, which they learned from Cézanne. To Cubism, their debt was equally profound, and not only because of their use of large, flat planes identified with that style. In Cubism, value changes (light to dark) did not function as they always had since the Renaissance. They did not suggest roundness or three-dimensionality, but projected instead a two-dimensional quality. Once painters like Russell and Macdonald-Wright had understood this important artistic development, it was but a short step for them to think of color as an entity in itself, no longer restricted to defining objects, an entity capable of being manipulated for non-objective effects. Color could, they realized, by itself suggest flatness, space, the juxtaposition of shapes, or emotional feelings. Far from being an offshoot of Cubism and little else, Orphism and Synchromism worked out Cubism's implications for the non-objective use of color. In 1913, few artists grasped this possibility; Russell and Macdonald-Wright did.

During the crucial years of Synchromism's development, from 1913 to 1918, Russell's style differed considerably from Macdonald-Wright's (*Ills. 10–5 and 10–6*). Russell applied color of equal intensity all over his canvas, thus activating the entire surface. When he changed a green from a light green to a dark one (a value change), he did not subtly model the alteration but indicated it boldly. The lighter green, therefore, does not appear to advance in front of the darker one. Rather, both greens assert their own individuality and cling with equal strength to the picture plane. Depth is, therefore, denied. Macdonald-Wright, on the other hand, varied the intensity of colors, allowing

10–5. STANTON MACDONALD-WRIGHT, *"Oriental." Synchromy in Blue-Green,*
1918.

some to become strong while leaving others quite pale. Therefore, some
shapes emerge and others recede. (In traditional art, this is one method
of achieving atmospheric perspective.) The greater interest in movement through space was further enhanced by carefully gradated value
changes in many of his forms. Russell was closer to the most advanced
European sensibility; Macdonald-Wright retained an allegiance to the
older Cézannesque concept of space, and, in so doing, also to the very
American sense of distance and openness that dates back to the early
nineteenth century. In fact, one may even go so far as to say that in the
years between 1913 and 1915, no painter got his canvases as "flat" as
Russell did.

John Marin's confrontation with European art was neither as cere-
bral nor as technical as were those of the Synchromists, and perhaps

202

10–6. MORGAN RUSSELL, *Synchromy,* 1914–15.

for this reason he was sustained by his sources of inspiration for his entire lifetime. He always returned, as he said, to the sky, the sea, the mountains, and the plains "to sort of retrue himself up." [9]

While abroad from 1905 to 1911 (except for a brief return trip in 1910) he traced the steps, as others had done, through Neo-Impressionism, finally arriving at his mature style by 1910. Nothing in his previous work seems to have prepared him, or the subsequent viewer, for it. From Whistlerian city scenes, he moved to descriptions of the city

10-7. JOHN MARIN, *Brooklyn Bridge*, 1910.

as a twentieth-century organism, bursting with movement and life (*Ill. 10–7*).

He did not portray the city's intimate aspects as Henri did, nor did he try to paint the city as an idea. To "copy a seen object or a mind object . . . is wrong," he said. Instead, he painted "street and city movements as I feel them in such a way that what appears on the paper shall have a life of its own akin to the movements felt." [10] He piled, as he said, buildings on top of buildings and saw great forces at work in them, "the warring of the great and the small; influences of one mass on another greater or smaller mass. While these powers are at work pushing, pulling, sideways, downwards, upwards, I can hear the sound of their strife and there is great music being played." [11] He read the city for its total impact on his senses.

His splintered images remind one of Marin's French contemporary Robert Delaunay's Eiffel Tower series, begun in the same year as the *Brooklyn Bridge*. Marin's vocabulary, however, is closer to, though not identical with, the vocabulary of the Futurists. In fact, he might even have read Filippo Marinetti's first manifesto of Futurism published in *Le Figaro* in 1909 when he was in Paris. In any event, by 1910, he was able to erect on a Cubist scaffold a Fauvelike heightened visual response, which he then described in language a Futurist might have used.

But his work never became European in the same way that Weber's or the Synchromists' did. Marin's work retains to a greater degree the impact of actual visual experience. Painting became a means for sustaining intimate contact with the physical world rather than an exercise in reconstructing a scene's essential character. Although his work was often compared to that of Cézanne, Marin cared little for the Frenchman and his art, finding him to be a painter uninvolved with life. Marin also found fault with Mondrian for the same reason, believing that as fine as they were, nothing grew on the Dutchman's verticals and horizontals.

Marin recorded his intimate and momentary feelings quickly because, like Prendergast and Homer, he often used watercolors. Perhaps because of his speedy notations, his sense of structure was sometimes uncertain. To control it, he began to add bars of color to his paintings in the early 1920's (*Ills. 10–8 and 10–9*). These bars helped

10–8. JOHN MARIN, *Lower Manhattan*, 1920.

10–9. JOHN MARIN, *Pertaining to Stonington Harbor, Maine, no. 4*, 1926.

stabilize the shapes on the canvas, whose flatness Marin insisted on respecting. He did not mind, as he said, a good fight between three-dimensional and flattened forms, but in the end he did strive for an equilibrium between movement and stasis as well as pattern and depth. With the bars, his paintings seem to be composed of superimposed sections or compartmentalized episodes, and as a result they often project a Cubist stability.

Marin first visited the Maine coast in 1914, and though he visited other parts of the country, he returned there almost yearly until his death. There he certainly found elemental forces of nature and there he also learned to appreciate the abrupt contrasts one finds at the shore —between smooth sails and rough water, warm textures and cool surfaces. His was a happy vision that responded positively to the chaotic movements of sea and sky. He did not probe very far beneath surface excitement, being content to treat the forces of nature as generative ideas, and his paintings seem to reflect a process of amiable evolution. His rapid-fire brushstrokes suggest a pleasant world of becoming (*Ill. 10–10, and see 8–11*).

10–10. JOHN MARIN, *Lobster Boat,* 1940.

10–11. ARTHUR DOVE, *Sentimental Music,* 1917.

Arthur Dove cast that world in more precisely biological terms, and by virtue of his manipulation of forms often gave it strong sexual overtones. He dug farther into the core beneath the appearance that Marin saw. Of his first abstraction, done in 1910, he said that he "gave up trying to express an idea by stating innumerable little facts." [12] (Marin, on the other hand, persisted in stating them.)

208

Nevertheless, Dove's paintings are nature-bound. As Paul Rosenfeld has remarked, all of his work communicates some love and direct sensuous feeling for the earth.[13] Abroad in 1906 and 1907, Dove settled on a farm in Connecticut in 1910 where, he subsequently related, he had a Ryderlike revelation.[14] By choosing three forms from the planes on the sides of the trees on a hillside, and three colors, plus black and white, he was able to create a series of paintings that to him expressed the spirit of the whole hillside. This was achieved by discovering first the special "condition of light" unique to each object, and then a color that established the object in his mind. Finally, he found a "condition of form" typical of the object. In time, dependence on the object disappeared, as the means of expression became purely subjective. Because his point of departure was nature, he might be called a biomorphic abstractionist (*Ill. 10–11*).

Throughout his career, he was much concerned with the use of lines, employing them as perimeters, as planes, or as force lines penetrating objects (*Ill. 10–12*). A useful tool in collages he made during the mid-

10–12. ARTHUR DOVE, *Plant Forms*, 1915.

10–13. ARTHUR DOVE, *Goin' Fishin'*, 1925.

10–14. ARTHUR DOVE, *Sunrise, Number 3*, 1937.

10–15. GEORGIA O'KEEFFE, *Black Iris,* 1926.

1920's (*Ill. 10–13*), they also suggest the automatic brushstrokes of Surrealism. In the 1930's and 1940's, Dove's subject matter extended beyond plants and trees. He turned to basic, universal themes denoted by sunrise, moon, and time cycles, often couching them in obvious sexual metaphors, as if life and living were reducible to sexual principles (*Ill. 10–14*). In part, this approach was inspired by Stieglitz and the group around him, which found true liberation through liberation of the senses (a theme that was, however, also constantly reiterated in novels of the teens and twenties and, indeed, was one of the credos shared by all the arts of this period).

In those years, Georgia O'Keeffe's paintings were highly regarded for their essential femininity. As an artist, as Stieglitz's wife, and as a subject for his camera, her femaleness could not be forgotten, and she came to symbolize the overthrow of the old Puritan ethic. Although her own imagery was at times obvious and voluptuous, her technique was dry, even tight (*Ill. 10–15*). Like Dove, she emphasized the generative forces of nature and, when she moved to New Mexico in the 1920's, the arid sky bleached and pared her forms. These, which have filled entire canvases or have been small elements in paintings that suggest vast spaces, were, as Marsden Hartley once suggested, "mysteries from the garden." [15] They evoke nature; they do not describe it.

Like Washington Allston's generation, which tried to import an elevated foreign style to America, this one did not often meet with worldly success as it attempted to bring modern art to America. But the artists felt much less despair, even though the public cared little for their efforts. These artists did not court the public and had little antagonism toward it. Collectors could be found, and, in their own community, they found a certain security. They had learned to be outsiders, but they were not yet ready to abandon the country. If anything, they saw themselves in the vanguard of its artistic and social renewal. They accepted its basic ideals and used themes taken from the American landscape as springboards for their art. The legacy of Emerson and Whitman still ran deep. In view of then contemporary European attitudes of despair and disgust with society, one almost wants to question their right to such optimism.

It is no wonder, then, that the arrival in this country of such Dada artists as Marcel Duchamp and Francis Picabia initially had so little impact. Picabia visited New York in 1915 and again in 1917; Duchamp was there from 1915 to 1919 and again after 1920. They became well known, met many artists, but generated little enthusiasm for their art. Some years before his untimely death in 1918, Morton Schamberg, who had earlier written of modern art with great regard and painted accordingly, began experimenting with Dada techniques and subject

10–16. MORTON L. SCHAMBERG, *Telephone*, 1916.

matter, but rarely went as far as Duchamp (*Ill. 10–16*). Man Ray, who had conceived of a type of Dada art as early as 1911, found his attitude reinforced by the presence of the Europeans in New York. In their paintings, however, Schamberg and Ray adhered largely to Cubist stylistic conventions, including flattened forms, shallow spaces, and fragmented images (*Ill. 10–17*).

But most American painters were still searching in modern art for positive qualities to apply to modern life and not for a means to express their revulsion from it. The lack of respect for all values, the urge to destroy, and the anarchic freedom of Dada were inimical to their tastes and beliefs, certainly to those around Stieglitz. When American painters turned a critical eye on society in the 1920's and later, it was less with the desire to destroy than to debunk. They could be disillusioned but they would still believe art a useful tool for societal renewal. Even the overwhelming sense of despair that gripped American artists in the late 1940's and early 1950's was couched in the rhetoric of rebirth and regeneration. American artists have been bitter and downcast, but they have not yet given up hope.

10–17. MAN RAY, *The Rope Dancer Accompanies Herself with Her Shadows,* 1916.

CHAPTER ELEVEN

Between the Wars

The twenty-year period between World War I and World War II was one of the richest and most turbulent in the history of American painting. The century's most popular and its most despised work dates from these years, a paradox that reflects the confusion still engendered by the art of that era (*see Ill. 11-10*). Varieties of abstraction flourished, but the inter-war period was marked by a decided swing to realism. Although the businessman governments of Harding, Coolidge, and Hoover encouraged trade with European nations, and many Americans (as in previous decades) became expatriates, there developed in the 1920's a growing disenchantment with European affairs that reached unprecedented heights during the 1930's. The Red Scare of 1919, the immigration restriction laws of 1922, the execution of Sacco and Vanzetti in 1927, the anti-evolution crusade, and the rise of the Ku Klux Klan were symptoms of America's revulsion from the European involvement necessitated by World War I. Fewer artists experimented with modern Parisian modes, and many made a point of declaring their independence from the modern styles.

Artists of varying realist persuasion developed further the ideas of Robert Henri and his circle. They found in the countryside essential American experiences, not just pleasant views. They sought an American spirit and style in rural and suburban areas, and found an older America that was fast disappearing. Some, like Thomas Hart Benton, mourned the loss and tried to re-create it as popular myth; others, like Edward Hopper, were left numb by it. Few could let it go easily—fear of the present, evidently, being too strong to face with equanimity.

Other realists such as Ben Shahn developed Henri's interest in humanity beyond the level of personal relationship to that of social commentary. These painters believed that art should convey a message or be instructive. During a period when totalitarianism was on the rise and democratic economies were disintegrating, these artists committed themselves to public causes, avoiding, as they might have said, the luxury of seclusion in the studio or in the cornfields back home.

Some artists, like the Precisionists, tried to accommodate avant-garde tendencies to traditional realism, while still others worked in modern European modes. These artists tended to favor an analytical and geometric art, and even though many felt that their art could be used for social improvement,[1] they were severely criticized by their realist brethren.

All, however, were supported by various governmental programs devised to help artists survive the Depression. Of the four major programs, the two most important were the Section of Painting and Sculpture in the Treasury Department (1934–43), which was responsible for securing the best available American art for public buildings, and the Federal Art Project of the Works Progress Administration (1935–43), a multipurpose relief organization. The attitudes that governed large-scale federal support for the arts, a dream that Trumbull and Morse had once tried to bring life over a century before, only emphasized the nativist and socially committed tendencies already developing in American art since the 1920's.

The Precisionists, known also as the Immaculates and Cubist-Realists, began to define a style before 1920. They never actually formed a school, issued a manifesto, held group exhibitions, or even shared a specific program. But in the paintings of Charles Demuth, Charles Sheeler, and others the Roaring Twenties were hushed in similar ways.

As early as 1917, Demuth had begun to explore the subject matter and to develop the style identified with Precisionism (*Ill. 11–1*). Employing mechanical, industrial, and domestic forms, he groomed the environment so that it became an impersonal presence purged of human intimacy. The warming touches of accidental light, time, texture, or atmosphere were not allowed to intrude. Objects were seen with a fundamental clarity, but had no mass. Attracted by the industrial landscape, Demuth did not celebrate it. The positive appreciation of its life and imagery, so much in evidence before World War I, is not manifest in his work, nor in that of Sheeler. Buoyant enthusiasm, in the 1920's, had given way to a sullenness of mood and a refined aestheticism that approached the landscape on tip-toe (*see Ills. 9–12, 10–7, and 11–2*).

I I–I. CHARLES DEMUTH, *Paquebot Paris, ca.* 1922.

The disembodied facts were presented in a style that combined realism and Cubo-Futurism. This modified modernity would seem to have been an attempt to harmonize American literalness with abstract art, since it had stylistic sources in nineteenth-century landscapes, Shaker furniture, the mechanical forms of Duchamp (an artist well known to Demuth and Sheeler), and photography. What gives these paintings their particular American flavor is not necessarily their obvious American subject matter, but the way in which the modern painting techniques were used. In general, the Americans did not conceive of a painting as a series of interrelated forms which also identified specific objects. Rather, they first envisioned specific objects, which they then abstracted, thus betraying their underlying attachment to fact. In *Modern Conveniences* (*Ill. 11–2*), a Cubo-Futurist grid is imposed upon the building. The structure does not grow from a series of abstract forms.

The insistence of the Precisionists on American subject matter (paralleled in the literature of the period) was a response to the need for new interpretations in a rapidly changing society. In his paintings of

11–2. CHARLES DEMUTH,
Modern Conveniences,
1921.

11–3. CHARLES DEMUTH, *My Egypt,* 1927.

industrial themes, Demuth depicts factories that are already decaying totems in a dried-out environment. And even these can find an ancestry in nothing earlier than old silos, one of which Demuth painted and entitled *My Egypt* (*Ill. 11–3*). Like the hero of Edith Wharton's *Hudson River Bracketed* (1928), who found in an old house on the river an embodiment of the past, Demuth found his images within the context of an American history made both instant and prematurely aged. The implicit satire is not as innocent as it might seem, for the American past was one to which American artists responded with equal amounts of love and hate (*see Ills. 11–3, 11–6, and 11–10*). It was there and it furnished the artist with real or imagined roots that he frequently chose to recognize but not appreciate.

Like Demuth, Charles Sheeler developed a simplified vision of reality within a generic Cubist framework, but was even more responsive to individual objects. They exist—whole and integral—in his paintings, and because their basic shapes are emphasized, their reality seems intensified (*Ills. 11–4 and 11–5*).

Trained both at the School of Industrial Art in Philadelphia and,

11–4. CHARLES SHEELER, *American Landscape*, 1930.

11–5. CHARLES SHEELER, *Interior,* 1926.

with Demuth, at the Pennsylvania Academy of the Fine Arts, Sheeler first learned to paint under William Merritt Chase, an artist whose work exhibits notably fluent brushwork and brilliant finish. Not until 1929 did he eliminate the last vestiges of Chase's influence, a process that began as early as 1909. By the time he created the series of works derived from studies of the Ford automobile plant in Michigan (*see Ill. 11–4*), his mature style was fully formed. In the succeeding decades, his style became more abstract as he tended increasingly to transform the solid surfaces of buildings into transparent planes that hover over rather than rest upon the ground.

It was not simply Sheeler's love of Shaker furniture nor his skill as a photographer that give his work qualities that can be found in earlier American realistic styles, but his own intrinsic approach to art. Just as Ralph Earl domesticated international portraiture, so Sheeler Americanized twentieth-century modernism. Like Asher B. Durand, he favored "the picture which arrives at its destination without evidence of a trying journey rather than the one which shows the marks of the battle." [2] Even in his paintings that have a modern iconography, the past always lurks near the surface, and constantly threatens to overtake it.

Edward Hopper was both less modern and less tied to the past than Sheeler. By giving weight to mass by a more thorough modeling, his focus has not the laser precision of Sheeler's. His colors approximate those of reality, and his sense of space is traditional. He left natural what Sheeler made geometrical. Hopper drew his subject matter neither from modern industry nor from American artifacts, but, as often as not, from that old broken-down place called home. He painted the faded elegance of Victorian mansions and the harsh light that gives old neighborhoods a dilapidatedly clean look, and then detached them from our own time and life by railroad tracks or fences that separate the viewer from the buildings (*Ill. 11–6*). Although he was writing about the painter Charles Burchfield, Hopper aptly described himself as well when he said that Burchfield captured "all the sweltering, tawdry life of the American small town, and behind all, the sad desolation of our suburban landscapes." [3]

Hopper described an America drained of ebullient spirits. A student of Henri from about 1900 to about 1906, he rejected the realists'

11–6. EDWARD HOPPER, *House by the Railroad*, 1925.

virtuoso style and emotional outbursts as he portrayed the shriveling, crushing narrowness of small town and city (*Ill. 11–7, and see Ill. 9–16*). His paintings remind one of Theodore Dreiser's statement "It was wonderful to discover America but it would have been more wonderful to lose it." [4] For Dreiser as for Hopper, this was, of course, impossible.

Hopper's style and his attitude were fixed as early as 1908, and he spent the remainder of his career carrying out his chief aim in painting. It was to make "the most exact transcription possible of my most intimate impressions of nature." [5] In these transcriptions he glorified the banal and occasionally turned emptiness hopefully into fullness, but more often he left it as he found it. Where Thomas Cole had envisioned the still-virgin hills of America populated with heavenly mansions, Hopper showed the lower-middle-class streets that actually were to trudge over them (*Ill. 11–8, and see Ill. 6–5*). He painted, to use William Carlos Williams' image, the "beauty of the terrible faces of our nonentities." [6]

Few artists so savagely portrayed those faces as Grant Wood, an artist

11–7. EDWARD HOPPER, *Room in New York,* 1932.

11–8. EDWARD HOPPER, *Sunday,* 1926.

11–9. GRANT WOOD, *Daughters of Revolution*, 1932.

whose cornfed popular image belies the desperate criticism implicit in the paintings he completed just after the Crash of 1929 (*Ills. 11–9 and 11–10*). Chronologically, his subjects could easily have been the grandchildren of Bingham's river boatmen. Instead of perpetuating and developing the spirit and ideals reflected in the nineteenth-century paintings, Wood's figures have been imprisoned by them. The couple in *American Gothic* are locked within their cultural pretensions, attested to by their doubtless flinty religion and by the flimsy Gothic Revival house that seems to deny human warmth. The man and his wife are dead spirits. Like the country in which they are living, they, too, have lost their bearings.

The *Daughters of Revolution*, a calculated attack on the Daughters of the American Revolution, clings stubbornly to the past, cunningly symbolized by Leutze's famous painting in the background. The older work, which incarnates the bravery and daring of the Revolutionary War, is the heritage of the descendants who pose in front. But these are tea-sipping ladies with aristocratic airs and hardening of the arteries. For Wood, as for Hopper, America seemed to be a country prematurely

225

11–10. GRANT WOOD, *American Gothic,* 1930.

aged. The ease with which Eastman Johnson could move among such people was no longer possible (*see Ill. 7–15*). Within a fifty-year period, the American artist had grown apart from a large segment of his public, and even if he tried to honor it by accepting its values, the intervening years and the advent of foreign styles had changed his relationship too profoundly for the reunion of a prodigal son. Willy-nilly, the American artist had become a bohemian, cut off from the main body of society. He could try to effect changes in the nation's social and political outlook, or, as the modernists did, to point the way to a society of the future, or exclude all but the immediate problems of art. In any event, he was on the outside, and only by an act of will could he begin to reflect the tastes and attitudes of the ordinary person.

Along with Thomas Hart Benton and John Steuart Curry, Wood was one of the leading members of the Regionalist movement during the 1930's. The use of the word Regionalism in the art world owed much to the argumentative writings of the critic Thomas Craven, who favored Benton, Curry, and Wood above all other painters; but Regionalism did not encompass a style nor even a single point of view. It was simply an art that grew from local or national experiences. It was opposed to colonial dependency on European styles and attitudes and called for the final emergence of an American art. Many nativists and cosmopolitans believed that this would happen in the Middle West, that part of the country with a modicum of culture that had not been affected by European currents. The Regionalists were borne along on the national tide of self-documentation: The country was scrutinizing itself as never before, and governmental policies were becoming geared to aiding individuals and sections of the nation as well as the usual special-interest groups. If Regionalism often reduced to the level of retrospective back-fence gossip the spiritual experiences sought in the landscape by the Hudson River School, it demonstrated that in the twentieth century one really could not go home again.

But the Regionalists were not necessarily flag-waving conservatives. Wood was a New Deal Democrat and Benton was a latter-day Populist. Benton's political beliefs in part dictated his choice of subject matter. Deeply committed to an America that was still significantly affected by its recent frontier past, and also very concerned with the activities of people rather than the evolution of abstract ideas, he developed a complex art that tried to tell the history of America, both rural and urban, in a manner that can be best expressed as tabloid. If Hopper painted the lower middle class, Benton painted as one of them. His work was the latest assertion of the type of art developed by Mount and Bingham.

Benton saw America as a place of impelling dynamic energy. Everything in his paintings moves and gyrates. He developed a style aimed at capturing the speed and action that had transformed the country from frontier land to industrial giant in his own lifetime. Although well aware of modern European art (he had been a Synchromist before World War I), he preferred to work in a realistic style. For the murals about contemporary life in America he created for the New School for Social Research in New York, he even devised a realistic equivalent of Cubism that was modeled on nineteenth-century magazine illustrations as well as rotogravure sections of newspapers (*Ill. 11-11*). Rather than superimpose forms to suggest movement through time and space, he juxtaposed them, interrupting the sequences by

11–11. THOMAS HART BENTON, *City Scenes*, 1930.

means of architectural bars that suggested a Marin painting gone rigid. Such works were, in effect, modern panoramas presenting information about topography, industry, and customs in different parts of the country.

Benton had painted mural studies all through the 1920's and was one of those who helped create a climate of opinion favorable to large-scale painting during the 1930's. Another moving force was the Mexican mural renaissance led by Diego Rivera, José Clemente Orozco, and David Alfaro Siqueiros, three artists who were resident in America just before and after 1930. Their effect on the American scene was more immediate and temporarily more profound than that of Duchamp and Picabia some fifteen years before. Not only did their desire to produce a monumental and national art parallel Benton's own, but their ideological position influenced a generation of politically left-wing American painters who came to see in art a tool of social criticism and even political indoctrination.

Without the combination of an unprecedented economic depression and the Mexican influence, there probably would not have been an art of social realism in the country. Never before and never since have American artists been so acutely aware of social problems, so political minded, and so willing to turn their art to the service of social issues. Public-spirited as never before, they pictured themselves as citizens of the entire country, not just of an artistic community, and they wanted to further in their way the renewal of America. In the history of American painting, their art is unique.

Pinpointing the evils they found about them in the capitalist system, they fought (some literally) for economic modifications through such organizations as the American Artists Congress, founded in 1936, and in the various federal programs. Many found answers in Communism, but Social Realism did not so much enclose artists within a doctrinaire philosophy as provide them with a liberating humanitarianism with which to portray their life and time. Many Social Realists, themselves recent arrivals from Europe, painted alternately the stark reality of America in the 1930's and the dreams Europeans had held of America across the centuries (*Ills. 11–12 and 11–13*).

The Social Realists were clustered in New York. During the 1930's, their art grew primarily from the tradition of militant cartooning in

11–12. BEN SHAHN, *Scott's Run, West Virginia,* 1937.

11–13. BEN SHAHN, mural in the Community Center, Roosevelt, New Jersey, 1937–38.

11–14. BEN SHAHN, *The Passion of Sacco and Vanzetti*, 1931–32.

left-wing journals such as *The Masses, The Liberator,* and *The New Masses.* As in earlier twentieth-century American movements, no single style crystalized, but a general expressionistic flavor characterizes most of the work of the Social Realists.

Ben Shahn helped define the stylistic thrust and political context of Social Realism with his studies of the Sacco and Vanzetti trial and its aftermath (*Ill. 11–14*). He returned to America in 1929 from a two-year stay abroad and, like many other artists, found that modern French styles had lost their viability as a means of communication. Shahn once said that he had always wanted to live during the time of a great public event such as the Crucifixion, and he found one in the execution of the two men in 1927. He then turned his attention to social themes such as the problems facing immigrants and their useful absorption into American life (*see Ill. 11–13*).

Not every Social Realist painting had a social message, although a working-class bias is evident in most of them. The urban waterfront that had appeared in earlier American paintings as a park or a symbol of twentieth-century power became, in the work of men like Philip Evergood, a ramshackle, poverty-stricken place (*Ill. 11–15, and see Ills. 9–15 and 10–1*). For him, there was no poetry in poverty, only debasement. He felt "that you have to know humanity at the time you live. You can't just sit down at a desk and write a *Nana* unless you've lived it, by God, unless you've damn well sat in a cold basement half the night with down-and-outers and felt their suffering. And to me it meant even more. It meant fighting for them politically, besides putting it down on canvas."[7] Edward Hopper had already delineated the people mentally if not physically pulverized by the economic system, but Evergood went further and painted the symbols of that oppression, the mill, the workers' quarters, and the executive mansion on the hill (*Ill. 11–16*).

An able poet and fantasist, Evergood could not escape the demands the era made on his conscience, nor could the Regionalists. Both groups felt compelled to participate in the daily life of the people and in the aspirations of their country. Their needs reached beyond art alone, and it was the intense awareness of these needs that provided the art of the 1930's with a sense of unity and gave it a distinctive profile. These were grandly and triumphantly celebrated at the end of the decade, fittingly

11–15. PHILIP EVERGOOD, *The Old Wharf*, 1934.

11–16. PHILIP EVERGOOD, *Through the Mill*, 1940.

enough at opposite ends of the continent: at the New York World's Fair and the Golden Gate International Exposition in 1939–40.

The celebrations occurred just in time, for in the following years the world caught up with American art. During the international conflict, nationalist values lost currency. Humanitarian interests had, after all, done little to ward off one of the most brutal wars in the history of mankind; moreover, after the fall of Paris, American artists felt they must to some degree assume the responsibility for maintaining and continuing the course of Western art. The realistic art of the 1930's had been born in a time of economic tragedy and died in one of international human grief.

Although the years between the wars were characterized by an increasing realism and an anti-European bias, Americans were not oblivious to the School of Paris. During the 1930's, Hans Hofmann brought it to the attention of students in California and New York. He favored an expressive approach to abstract art, but an alternate view was held by a number of painters who subsequently formed the American Abstract Artists in 1936. Theirs was a harder-edged, more mathematically oriented world of rational discourse in which "the bare expressiveness of shape and position of shape must be pondered anew; the weight of color, the direction of line and angle can be restudied until the roots of primary tactile reaction shall be perceived again" (*Ill. 11–17*). [8]

The differences between men like Benton, Shahn, and George L. K. Morris, a chief spokesman and painter among the abstractionists, were not as unbridgeable as the partisan politics of art of the time might indicate. At least one major figure surmounted them, Stuart Davis. His paintings not only reflected styles and themes available at home, they also recorded what Americans saw and borrowed from abroad. His work is that of an American confidently rooted in his own country, but international in outlook. By avoiding parochialism on the one hand and sycophantic adulation of European styles on the other, and by contributing his energies to political causes, he may well come to be regarded a hundred or so years hence as *the* American painter most representative of the first half of the twentieth century. As he said, in more than one context, "I want to paint and do paint particular aspects of this country which interest me. But I use, as a great many others do,

234

11–17. GEORGE L. K. MORRIS, *Nautical Composition,* 1937–42.

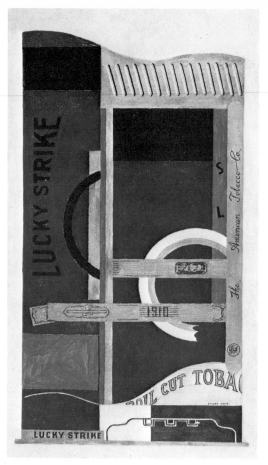

some of the methods of modern French painting which I consider to have universal validity." [9]

In his mature works, done as early as 1917, he took the bright colors of Fauve and Orphist paintings and married them to compositional techniques based on Cubist collage devices of discontinuous, overlapping, and superimposed forms. By emphasizing colors equally across a canvas and by giving minor details the same degree of amplification as major ones (a stylistic combination not found in most European art) Davis created forms that seem to push out against a canvas's perimeter. His ability to suggest a larger landscape beyond the frame recalls

Hudson River School and Luminist paintings. In his use of harsh, opaque colors and an open construction, Davis also developed a style peculiarly American in its brashness and raw poster-paint quality.

An early painting, *Lucky Strike* (*Ill. 11–18*), one of a series based on tobacco motifs, reflects a Dadaist regard for unartistic materials as subject matter. However, the precision of detail and the carefully wrought illusionism owes more to native American sources than to, say, Kurt Schwitters, the European collagist. "Some felt they could jump right in and paint a cubist picture," Davis said. "I couldn't. I could only keep looking at a manageable hunk of the world and keep trying to twist and shape it my way. I wanted something solid, so I picked out *things* instead of *manners*." [10]

Because of his concern for things, he transcribed rather than transformed his subjects. His *Town Square* (*Ill. 11–19*), like an optical illusion, can turn as mysterious as a painting by the proto-Surrealistic De Chirico. The gasoline pumps become metaphysicians and poets, the spaces are quickly receding journeys into Italian landscape. But then,

11–19. STUART DAVIS, *Town Square*, 1925–26.

11–20. STUART DAVIS, *Swing Landscape,* 1938.

one inevitably returns to the facts and sees nothing more than objects in an American landscape—no mystery, no surreal incantation, only a rural town square.

Through the 1930's, while participating in many causes allied with Social Realist art, Davis continued to paint works that offer a balance between recognizable imagery and complete abstraction. Like Bellows, Marin, and Benton, he, too, desired to capture the visual excitement offered by land- and cityscapes but, as he said, "not in the sense of describing them in graphic images, but by predetermining an analogous dynamics in the design, which becomes a new part of the American environment." [11] One of the most important paintings suggesting analogous dynamics and one that looked back to open-ended Luminist landscapes and forward to Abstract Expressionist paintings was *Swing Landscape (Ill. 11–20),* a work that seems to push out at its seams. Neither a retrospective nor a clinical elaboration of forms, it evokes a contemporary America by means of a color-space composition, a phrase Davis often used to indicate the process of transferring to canvas objects in the American environment and his feelings about both the objects and the environment.

238

11–21. STUART DAVIS, *Visa,* 1951.

In his later years, Davis worked largely within the framework of Cubist collage, undoubtedly aware of the late works of Matisse and the paintings of Josef Albers, the color theorist who came to America from the Bauhaus before World War II. But, typically, he reinterpreted their findings, energizing them with strong clashes of complementary color, printed words, and cruder forms as well as emphatic detail (*Ill. 11–21*). Although we no longer recognize it as such, his work stands in the same relation to European art as, say, Ralph Earl's did over a century before. What had once been considered provincial, however, had now become recognized as American.

CHAPTER TWELVE

To the Present

By 1940, a younger generation no longer found the moods and modes of the 1930's viable. Emigré European artists, from Surrealists such as André Breton and André Masson to rigid Non-Objectivists like Mondrian, were settling in and near New York. The new world war had begun to have a telling effect. The times, in the eyes of young American painters, were times of crisis and choice.

As New York became the world's international art center, painting in America increasingly shed its parochial flavor and sought inspiration in European culture. Instead of going abroad for training and seasoning, young Americans could for the first time study and observe Europe's leading artists on their own ground. They were able to keep a stronger grip on their artistic personalities and interpret the attitudes and theories of the Europeans in terms of their own experiences and environment immediately, not years later after they came home. Grimly aware of the devastation of Europe and with a growing realization that the postwar years would not necessarily be ones of easy recovery, American painters were in an excellent psychological and material position to assume the role of leadership in Western art.

In which direction would the young generation move? Influences abounded. In retrospect, the choices seem inevitable; at the time, they did not.[1] What could artists paint after the total mobilization of some countries and the extensive destruction of others? Or after the calculated murder of fantastic numbers of people? What was meaningful in a world where sanity seemed a perversion and where decency was irrelevant? How and where could an individual take his stand?

Caught in an ethical dilemma concerning the significance of art and the value of their careers as artists, the nascent Abstract Expressionists found artistic release primarily in the example of the Surrealists such as Breton and Masson who provided techniques for exploring the instinctual, the irrational, and the interior vision as well as a means to develop a subject matter inspired by images and notions derived from primitive societies and protozoic forms (*see Ills. 12–2 and 12–7*). Disavowing modern Western culture, the artists wanted to start the world all over again, as it were. As Dore Ashton has said, "they were not trying to resurrect *specific* myths. What they attempted was to invest their images with the aura of myth, the atmosphere of mysterious ritual." [2]

They sought a new reality based on unpremeditated impulse, automatism, and immediate sensation. By 1950, many had even discarded the minimal thematic props of a few years before, embarking instead on an extended voyage to the center of their own selves, the ultimate source of renewal and regeneration. Such action affirmed their presence as unique creatures; or, at least, such withdrawal preserved the illusion of their individuality. As a result, the personal gesture and the individual sign became extraordinarily important as symbols of human engagement in a depersonalized age. The drip was not really a drip, but a desperate assertion of self. Like the most famous graffito-maker of those years, each artist became his own Kilroy: He was there. His art, as Harold Rosenberg has suggested, became "the means of confronting in daily practice the problematic nature of modern individuality." [3]

The Americans did not develop a fundamental philosophy, believing that engagement in the process of painting provided its own justification. Nevertheless, knowledge of Existentialism's significant assertions might have served as a source of encouragement in the first postwar years. In his essay on Existentialism, published in America in 1947, Jean-Paul Sartre stated, "There is no reality except in action. Man . . . exists only to the extent that he fulfills himself; he is therefore nothing else than the ensemble of his acts, nothing else than his life." [4] Understanding the finer points of Sartre's argument was not essential to the realization that each stroke on a canvas, each decision, was of the artist's own making. The canvas became the sum total of his acts, and no one else's.

This intense introspection, paradoxically, may have encouraged the public acceptance of Abstract Expressionism in the later 1950's, for as Emerson once reminded his audience in his essay "The American

Scholar" (1837), "the deeper [one] dives into his privatest, secretest presentiments, to his wonder he finds this is the most acceptable, most public, and universally true. The people delight in it; the better part of every man feels, This is my music; this myself." [5] The public enjoyed vicariously the Abstract Expressionists' freedom of choice and "secretest presentiments." In an era of mechanization and social facelessness, it recognized in these artists an affirmation of the old American myth of the self-sufficient pioneer and rugged individualist.

It was Jackson Pollock who best fit into the heroic image of Paul Bunyan and John Henry, archetypal Americans who possessed overwhelming amounts of raw energy, stamina, and lust for action—in whose mold were also cast, to a greater or lesser degree, Walt Whitman, George Bellows, and Thomas Wolfe. Pollock early absorbed the expressionism of José Clemente Orozco and Thomas Hart Benton (his teacher in the early 1930's) and, in the 1940's, the automatic devices of the Surrealists as he learned to channel the unruly forces that dominated his art.

During the 1940's, he explored the terrain of the prelogical but excluded bizarre Surrealist fantasy and literary symbolism. Vaguely totemic images, often suggestive of ritual, served as points of departure for authentic experience. This was found in the creation of the painting, of energy arcs, of amorphous shapes suggesting biological states of development, and in the immediate sensation of give-and-take between forms in development as they deployed themselves across the canvas (*Ill. 12–2*). As is true of much modern architecture, there is no governing conception of form and proportion, of identification and recognition of individual units in Pollock's work. What was front or side (façade or flank), object or area (door or wall), lost precise definition as a unit.

In its place were the hard facts of pigment and painting surface. Superposition of forms did not necessarily imply recession into space because forms and colors were not related in a spatially logical way. Adolph Gottlieb and Mark Rothko had asserted in 1943 that "We are for flat forms because they destroy illusion and reveal truth." [6] But revelation of truth was only part of it. Pollock's paintings probed the spatial limits that Cubism, with its interrelationships of field and figure, had clamped upon modern art. Pollock was looking into a space that

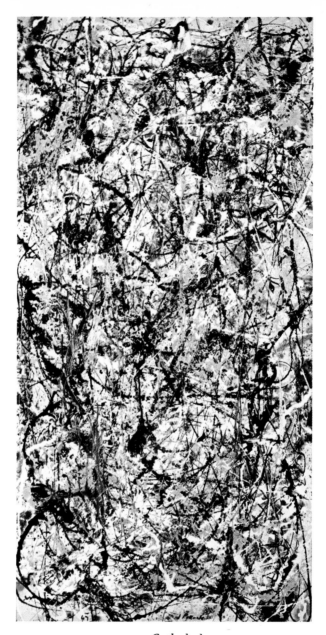

12–1. JACKSON POLLOCK, *Cathedral*, 1947.

existed in his mind. The space he saw was flattened, but more important, it was lacking in depth cues because it was so completely imaginary.

In the late 1940's, Pollock, like other painters, began to consider the unqualified act of painting itself (*Ill. 12–1*). His drip paintings, the first begun in 1947, were often placed on the floor, the better to record gestures larger than the swing of a wrist or of the hand. Of this method, Pollock said, "I feel nearer, more a part of the painting, since this way I can walk around it, work from the four sides and literally be *in* the painting." [7] His canvases became, in effect, the repository of those momentary responses emanating from the artist's mind and soul, physically translated into manual gestures, all of them modified by the sum total of the artist's understanding of his environment and his time. As Harold Rosenberg observed of Pollock and his contemporaries, the canvas appeared to them "as an arena in which to act—rather than as a space in which to reproduce, re-design, analyze or 'express' an object actual or imagined." [8]

In Pollock's paintings, forms push toward the outer limits of their

12–2. JACKSON POLLOCK, *Guardians of the Secret*, 1943.

boundaries and imply a lateral extension of space beyond. A feature of American painting since the Hudson River School, if not before, it was redefined by Pollock in terms of modern flux and change. He cast it in terms of the vocabulary of art itself—shapes, forms, and color, spatial allusions and contours—rather than of objects clearly defined. And the rawness and directness as well as the crudity of his attack gives these paintings an aspect foreign to modern European art.

To a certain extent, Willem de Kooning played a mediating role between European tradition and American spontaneity during the 1940's and 1950's. Trained in his native Holland before coming to America in 1926, he had a substantial knowledge of European procedures. Few men show so clearly in their work the struggle to break through Cubist spatial devices in order to be free for more personal experiments with space and color. In his various black-on-white and white-on-black studies done around 1950, de Kooning tried to destroy the idea of a figure in a field (*Ill. 12–3*). His methods included basing shapes on accidental assemblages of torn newspapers and cut-up drawings. These devices helped to create spatial jumps and open forms, and

12–3. WILLEM DE KOONING, *Painting,* 1948.

12–4. WILLEM DE KOONING, *Gotham News, ca.* 1955.

to prevent the reading of white shapes as lying on black ones, or vice-versa. They suggested the "no-environment" through which de Kooning then perceived the world.

In the finest of these abstract works, paintings such as *Gotham News* (*Ill. 12–4*), the central focal point that has almost always appeared in European art since the Renaissance is evident, as are the subordinate forms spaced around it. Yet, the energetic strokes, splashed colors, broken shapes, and crude finish bespeak new sources de Kooning tapped in America. But his continual return to the figure, particularly to the female form, and his willingness to allow the viewer to find in

246

his paintings themes of birth and destruction bespeak his European inheritance (*Ill. 12–5*). Given the different historical and social circumstances, he has acted a role in his generation not unlike Thomas Cole's in his, by fusing traditional European concerns for composition and complex subject matter with American openness and less complicated literary meanings.

Pollock and de Kooning emphasized the aspect of Abstract Expressionism that equated gesture with content. Others, like Hans Hofmann, effectively employed gesture and color to organize and contain forms (*Ill. 12–6*). Still others preferred to make color sensation a subject that was the equivalent of gesture. Mark Rothko was a major exponent of this tendency. In the 1940's, he, too, explored a quasi-mythic world, which in his case evoked dreams of protozoic beginnings on the shores of a new time (*Ill. 12–7*). By 1950, his shapes had broadened out and his colors expanded, incorporating ever-larger units so that, even if one still recognized in them "the principle and passion of organisms," they maintained "no direct association with any particular visible experience."[9] Ultimately, they became large bands, three and

12–5. WILLEM DE KOONING, *Woman I,* 1950–52.

12–6. HANS HOFMANN, *Smaragd Red and Germinating Yellow*, 1959.

12–7. MARK ROTHKO, *Baptismal Scene,* 1945.

four to a canvas, which hovered one above the other between ill-defined
margins (*Ill. 12–8*). Like Pollock, he eliminated depth cues, usually by
relating the sizes of his shapes and their colors and values so that they
would adhere as uniformly as possible to the picture surface. His forms
are flat but not inert.

Rothko's concern with the mystery and wonder of creation and his
reliance upon color to express them recall Washington Allston's early
outlook and experience. But Rothko concentrated on shape and color
relationships to the exclusion of all else. What one reads into Rothko's

12–8. MARK ROTHKO, *Red Maroons, 1962 #2,* 1962.

paintings depends on oneself; Allston always provided a point of departure. In a country where the exploration of color has tended to be neglected, Rothko has become one of its major colorists. His works of the 1950's and later are lush—a descriptive term hardly applicable to any earlier artist's paintings.

The artistic situation in the United States in the mid-1950's is loosely analogous to that of the mid-1880's in France. At that time, two tendencies emerged in reaction to Impressionism—a rationalist, constructive one, exemplified in the paintings of Seurat and Cézanne, and an emotional, expressive one, reflected in the works of Gauguin and Van Gogh. A similar but of course not identical pattern of reaction to, and development from, Abstract Expressionism can be discerned. Two general tendencies emerged—one toward a return to the figure and identifiable objects, the other toward the clearer definition of structure and color.

The figural direction was taken by a group of West Coast painters who combined Fauve color with the freedom of the Abstract Expressionist brushstroke to suggested individual response in the face of problematic human encounters (*Ill. 12–9*). Richard Diebenkorn expressed the feelings of many who had once studied under the postwar generation of artists when he said, "I came to mistrust my desire to explode the picture and supercharge it in some way." [10]

No doubt, the humanism of Diebenkorn, David Park, and others

12–9. RICHARD DIEBENKORN, *Woman in a Window*, 1957.

12–10. ROBERT RAUSCHENBERG, *White Painting,* 1951.

seemed old-fashioned to some artists of the same generation who
wanted to avoid the hurdles of the autobiographical statement. Instead
of exploring problematic human encounters, they preferred to explore
problematic artistic encounters by raising questions about the identity
and relevance of the art object, about the context in which a work
could be called art, about the possibility of presenting the most minimal
visual information necessary to define a work of art, and about the
type of stance on artistic issues viable in an era of nuclear diplomacy,
continuing war, decaying traditions, and growing automation. Although America and the world (the terms were becoming synony-
mous) still had much to offer, for many "the world [had become]
more a predicament than a spectacle" by the 1960's.[11]

Robert Rauschenberg considered the ramifications of these questions
during the 1950's and helped both to liberate younger artists from the
need to record their own experiences and to suggest new ways to
approach the problem of artistic expression. The main thrust of his
work involved "the tension between freely manipulated oil paint close
to the expressionist style of de Kooning, and real objects, almost in-

12–11. ROBERT RAUSCHENBERG, *Gloria,* 1956.

variably 'found' materials of great variety and in relative states of de-
cay." [12] As a real object, the canvas itself was included, and it could
be considered as a shape whole and complete in relation to other
shapes, or merely as a repository for color, or as an expression of the
void (*Ill. 12–10*).

In time, it became a receptacle, accepting on its surfaces not only
color but also other objects randomly found and given randomly assigned places with a minimum of artistic control (*Ill. 12–11*). Neither
secret messages nor meanings, except, perhaps, the most general com-

ments on the pace and style of contemporary society, were attached to his work. But, as have few other artists, Rauschenberg reflects the dilemmas of modern society. Although his collected objects have intrinsic meaning in their own right, their context is destroyed. Their juxtaposition with other objects suggests meaning too vague to pin down. His work is the equivalent of the Theater of the Absurd, which, as Marshall McLuhan has suggested, "dramatizes the recent dilemma of Western man, the man of action who appears not to be involved in the action." [13]

This McLuhanesque view of Western man became a basic tenet of Pop art, a style that flourished in the 1960's and took as its point of departure images appearing in the popular media, including comic strips, movie posters, and advertisements. Emotion and feeling were depicted less with tongue in cheek than simply at second hand. Pop images—comic strip heroines, movie queens, food, scenes of violence— are projected as if packaged for consumption rather than contemplation (*Ills. 12–12, 12–13, and 12–14*). The Pop sculptor Claes Oldenburg expressed the Pop artists' attitude when he said, "It is possible for me to treat my subjectivity and that of others objectively and this is a unique thing in my art: the emotion in it is the observation of emotion." [14] By making monumental the trivia of existence and exploring the leftover images of a technological society, the Pop artist, like modern man, would seem to have become "so routinized that the only mood that possesses him is complete dissociation." [15] The despair in the face of a materialistic and mechanized society that European artists like Kandinsky expressed earlier in the century at least did not exclude the possibility of individual action. Those artists felt themselves to be unique individuals capable of dealing with the world situation. The Pop artists suggested that there was no room for individual response.

The brashness of Pop art hid the malaise that lurked underneath. The look was usually hard-edged and bright-colored, with few complications of patterning or of color and value relationship. Its mechanized qualities were emphasized by Roy Lichtenstein, who once stated that "the meaning of my work is that it's industrial," and Andy Warhol, who said, "the reason I'm painting this way is that I want to be a machine, and I feel that whatever I do and do machine-like is what I want to do." [16]

12–12. ANDY WARHOL, *Campbell Soup Can 19¢*, 1960.

12–13. ROY LICHTENSTEIN, *Good Morning Darling*, 1964.

12–14. ANDY WARHOL, *Elvis,* 1964.

Pop artists invariably concentrated on individual components rather than whole units. The easy flow of gesture and time suggested in Abstract Expressionism was halted, even though occasionally Pop motifs were used repeatedly, as if cut from a strip of film (*see Ill. 12–14*). Yet this determined focusing developed out of Abstract Expressionism. Just as the Abstract Expressionist artist painted as he felt at the moment, the Pop artist painted what he saw at the moment. Neither concentrated on vast complex scenes of the mind or of the landscape. Instead, they narrowed their focus to either intimate states of feeling (Abstract Expressionism) or immediately perceivable, directly touchable objects (Pop art). Like their predecessors, Pop artists did not back off for the long view.

Artists who have given a more obvious sense of structure to nonobjective forms are called Op, Hard Edge, and Minimal artists. The boundaries between the types are, of course, nonexistent, and all three merge with groups such as the kinetic sculptors. With few exceptions, these painters employ carefully indicated forms and bright, saturated colors that suggest the cool precision of the machine. Op artists tend to emphasize coloristic relationships, often restricting their interest to the manipulation of physiological effects on the viewer as he perceives the edges of shapes whose colors clash or cooperate. Hard Edge painters explore to a greater extent relationships of shape and space. Like their Abstract Expressionist predecessors, all these artists maintain freedom of choice in selecting forms, although they do so to a lesser degree and do not emphasize physical gesture. As Al Held, a Hard Edge painter, once remarked, "I thought the two great poles—Mondrian, who represented objectivity, and Pollock, who represented supreme subjectivity—could be combined."[17]

Artists such as Frank Stella, Ellsworth Kelly, and Kenneth Noland developed further the object quality of paintings by Robert Rauschenberg. In fact, the meaning inherent in a Hard Edge painting is simply its presence as a painted object. These artists join the Pop painters in their withdrawal from firsthand experiences insofar as many of their paintings eschew tactility and embrace opticality. That is, given the absence of depth cues, one cannot even imagine entering the space of their paintings but can only observe them from the outside (*Ill. 12–15*). A Hard Edge painting should be viewed as a whole unit. The

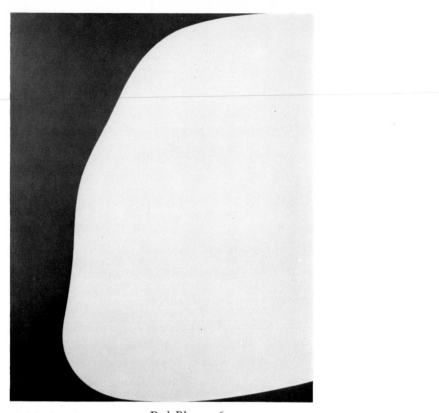

12–15. ELLSWORTH KELLY, *Red Blue*, 1962.

few large or repetitive forms should not interfere with perceiving the form of the canvas itself as an object. The painted surface is just that, an area between the framing edges. Colors and shapes are brought up to an equivalence so that none seem to advance or recede. The surface is a skin pulled tight.

Of the three painters mentioned, Stella is the most iconoclastic. He has let the stretcher determine the direction of the markings on his canvases as if their outer edges had unwound from their centers, and he has shaped his canvases and painted them as if they were relief sculpture (*Ill. 12–17*). He believes that a painting "really is an object.

12–16. KENNETH NOLAND, *Royal Drawl*, 1970.

Any painting is an object and anyone who gets involved enough in this finally has to face up to the objectness of whatever it is that he's doing." [18]

From the point of view of the history of American art, Noland is the most interesting, and, like Stuart Davis, he reveals how an international modern vocabulary can be Americanized. In his chevron paintings of the mid-1960's (*Ill. 12–18*), the chevrons pierce the canvas and seem to push out toward the edges (in a typical European solution, forms tend to collapse around a central focal point). But with the greater sophistication Americans have acquired over the years of exposure to modernism, Noland is able to make better use of his borders as containing edges rather than as edges over which the action and spaces seemingly splash. However, his paintings of the late 1960's and early 1970's revert to suggesting the run-on landscape (*Ill. 12–16*), indicating a lateral extension of the visual field.

Implicit in his work, and to greater or lesser degree in that of like-minded artists, is the continued dialogue between the American prefer-

12–17. FRANK STELLA, *Gran Cairo*, 1962.

ence for dry color and for recollections of the American environment, and the form conceptions of modern European art. The quality of expansiveness keenly felt in Noland's work does not seem an imposition on an essentially European conception of form but, rather, a natural outgrowth of that conception. It is this sense of expansiveness, observable first among the Abstract Expressionists, that marks the true domestication—not simply the acquisition—of modern art in America,

12–18. KENNETH NOLAND, *Morning Span, 1963.*

and the final catching up of American with European art. American painting, which began as an extension of European art, had, some three hundred years later, become at least the equal of it and, in the eyes of many, something more. Whether American painters can maintain their new position, continue to reflect current human conditions, and develop further the possibilities of their craft are of course open questions. But the indications are that they will.

Notes

CHAPTER 1

1. From Cotton Mather, *Magnalia Christi Americana* (London, 1702), I, as quoted in Thomas Jefferson Wertenbaker, *The Puritan Oligarchy* (New York: C. Scribner's Sons, 1947) p. 32.

2. Louis B. Wright, *The Cultural Life of the American Colonies* (New York: Harper and Row, 1957), p. 34.

3. Quoted in Eric Mercer, *English Art 1553–1625* (Oxford: Oxford University Press, 1962), p. 157.

CHAPTER 2

1. Waldron Phoenix Belknap, Jr., *American Colonial Painting: Materials for a History* (Cambridge: Harvard University Press, 1959), pp. 273 ff.

2. Frederick B. Tolles, "A Contemporary Comment on Gustavus Hesselius," *The Art Quarterly,* XVII (Oct.–Dec., 1953), 271–73.

3. Quoted in Jules David Prown, *John Singleton Copley* (Cambridge, Mass.: Harvard University Press, 1966), I, 45.

4. James Thomas Flexner, *First Flowers of Our Wilderness* (Boston: Houghton Mifflin, 1947), pp. 68–89.

5. Alan Burroughs, "Notes on Smibert's Development," *Art in America,* XXX (April, 1942), 109–21.

CHAPTER 3

1. George C. Groce, "John Wollaston: A Cosmopolitan Painter in the British Colonies," *The Art Quarterly,* 15 (Summer, 1952), 133.

2. Quoted in Jules David Prown, *John Singleton Copley,* I, 17.

3. Quoted in *ibid.,* II, 245.

4. Quoted in Louis Legrand Noble, *The Life and Works of Thomas Cole,* edited by Elliot S. Vessell (Cambridge, Mass.: Harvard University Press, 1964), p. 220.

5. Adolph Gottlieb, "The Artist and the Public," *Art in America,* LXII (Dec., 1954), 268.

6. Prown, *op. cit.,* I, p. 79.

1. From Michael Wigglesworth, "God's Controversy with New England" (1662), in *Proceedings of the Massachusetts Historical Society, 1871–73* (Boston: Massachusetts Historical Society, 1873), p. 83; and Timothy Dwight, "Greenfield Hill" (1794), in William J. McTaggart and William K. Bottorff (eds.), *The Major Poems of Timothy Dwight* (Gainsville, Fla.: Scholars' Facsimiles and Reprints, 1969), p. 418. See also Henry Nash Smith, *Virgin Land* (New York: Vintage Books, 1950), pp. 4, 11.

2. Neil Harris, *The Artist in American Society* (New York: George Braziller, 1966), Chapter II.

3. Quoted in William Dunlap, *A History of the Rise and Progress of the Arts of Design in the United States,* edited by Alexander Wyckoff (New York: Blom, 1965), III, 91–93.

4. Quoted in Jules David Prown, *John Singleton Copley,* II, 297.

5. John Trumbull, *Autobiography, Reminiscences and Letters* (New York: Wiley and Putnam, 1841), p. 159.

6. Russel Blaine Nye, *The Cultural Life of the New Nation* (New York: Harper and Row, 1960), pp. 42, 147–49.

7. Trumbull, *op. cit.,* pp. 339–40.

8. Harris, *op. cit.,* p. 47.

9. Quoted in Marcus Cunliffe, *The Literature of the United States* (Baltimore and London: Penguin Books, 1961), p. 40.

10. William Whitley, *Gilbert Stuart* (Cambridge, Mass.: Harvard University Press, 1932), pp. 56–59.

11. Quoted in Dunlap, *op. cit.,* I, 215–16.

12. Quoted in *ibid.,* p. 220.

13. Charles Coleman Sellers, *Charles Willson Peale* (Philadelphia: *Memoirs of the American Philosophical Society,* Vol. 23, No. 2, 1947), p. 224.

1. E. P. Richardson, *Washington Allston* (Chicago: University of Chicago Press, 1948), p. 175.

2. Washington Allston, *Lectures on Art, and Poems,* edited by Richard Henry Dana, Jr. (New York: Baker and Scribner, 1850).

3. Quoted in Richardson, *op. cit.,* p. 115.

4. Quoted in *ibid.,* pp. 59–60.

5. Quoted in William Dunlap, *A History of the Rise and Progress of the Arts of Design in the United States,* II, p. 313.

6. Quoted in James Thomas Flexner, *That Wilder Image* (Boston: Little, Brown, 1962), p. 48n.

7. Quoted in Oliver W. Larkin, *Samuel F. B. Morse and American Democratic Art* (Boston: Little, Brown, 1954), pp. 31–32.

8. *Ibid.,* p. 64.

1. Leon Howard, *Literature and the American Tradition* (New York: Doubleday, 1960), pp. 81–82.

2. Quoted in Russel Blaine Nye, *The Cultural Life of the New Nation*, p. 242.

3. Harold Edward Dickson (ed.), *Observations on American Art: Selections from the Writings of John Neal (1793–1876)* (State College, Pa.: Pennsylvania State College Studies, No. 12, 1943), p. 34.

4. Marcus Cunliffe, *The Nation Takes Shape 1789–1837* (Chicago: University of Chicago Press, 1959), p. 135.

5. Louis Legrand Noble, *The Life and Works of Thomas Cole*, p. xxiv.

6. Henry T. Tuckerman, *Artist-Life* (New York: D. Appleton and Co., 1847), p. 80.

7. *The Dial*, I (1841), p. 374.

8. Quoted in Louis Legrand Noble, *op. cit.*, pp. 281–82.

9. Quoted in *ibid.*, p. 169.

10. Alan P. Wallach, "Cole, Byron and *The Course of Empire*," *Art Bulletin*, L (Dec., 1968), 375–79.

11. From Thomas Cole, "Essay on American Scenery" (1836), as quoted in John W. McCoubrey (ed.), *American Art 1700–1960* (Englewood Cliffs, N.J.: Prentice-Hall, 1965), p. 106.

12. Published in *The Crayon*, I (1855), 34–35, 97–98.

13. John Filson, *Life and Adventures of Colonel Daniel Boon* [sic] . . . *written by himself* (Brooklyn: C. Wilder, 1823), p. 15.

1. Henry T. Tuckerman, *Book of the Artists* (New York: G. P. Putnam and Son, 1867), p. 409.

2. James Jackson Jarves, *The Art-Idea*, edited by Benjamin Rowland, Jr. (Cambridge, Mass.: Harvard University Press, 1960), p. 189.

3. Quoted in John K. Howat, *John Frederick Kensett 1816–1872* (New York: The American Federation of Arts, 1968), not paged.

4. Henry T. Tuckerman, *Artist-Life*, p. 88.

5. Quoted in John I. H. Baur, "American Luminism," *Perspectives USA*, No. 9 (Autumn, 1954), 93.

6. *Encyclopaedia Britannica*, eleventh edition, XIII, 875.

7. David Huntington, *The Landscapes of Frederic Edwin Church* (New York: George Braziller, 1966), pp. 78 ff.

8. Jarves, *op. cit.*, p. 180.

9. Quoted in Vernon Louis Parrington, *Main Currents in American Thought* (New York: Harcourt, Brace, 1954), p. 101.

10. George Inness, Jr., *The Life, Art and Letters of George Inness* (New York: The Century Co., 1917), p. 174.

11. *Ibid.,* p. 101.

12. Quoted in Elliott Daingerfield, *George Inness* (New York: privately printed, 1911), p. 54.

CHAPTER 8

1. Quoted in Frederic Fairchild Sherman, *Albert Pinkham Ryder* (New York: privately printed, 1920), p. 36.

2. Quoted in *ibid.,* p. 13.

3. Richard Braddock, "The Literary World of Albert Pinkham Ryder," *Gazette des Beaux-Arts,* 6th series, XXXIII (1948), 47–54.

4. "Sketches and Studies," *The Art Journal,* VI (1880), 107.

5. Lloyd Goodrich, *Winslow Homer* (Published for the Whitney Museum of American Art. New York: Macmillan, 1944), p. 53.

6. Henry Steele Commager, *The American Mind* (New Haven: Yale University Press, 1950), *passim.* See also Jay Martin, *Harvests of Change* (Englewood Cliffs: Prentice-Hall, 1967), pp. 7–10.

7. S. G. W. Benjamin, *Art in America* (New York: Harper and Brothers, 1880), p. 188.

8. John Fiske, *Outlines of Cosmic Philosophy* (Boston: Houghton Mifflin and Company, 1874), and Henry Ward Beecher, *Evolution and Religion* (New York: Fords, Howard, and Hulbert, 1886).

9. Quoted in Lloyd Goodrich, *Thomas Eakins* (New York: Whitney Museum of American Art, 1933), p. 40.

10. Quoted in *ibid.,* p. 40.

11. Charles S. Kessler, "The Realism of Thomas Eakins," *Arts Magazine,* XXXVI (Jan., 1962), 22.

CHAPTER 9

1. Robert Henri, "The New York Exhibition of Independent Artists," *The Craftsman,* XVIII (1910), 161.

2. Quoted in Mary Fanton Roberts, " 'Painting Real People' Is the Purpose of George Luks' Art," *The Touchstone,* VIII (Oct., 1920), 35.

3. Louis Baury, "The Message of Proletaire," *The Bookman,* XXXIV (December, 1911), 400–13.

4. Quoted in Alfred Kazin, *On Native Grounds* (New York: Doubleday, 1956), p. 75.

5. Robert Henri, *The Art Spirit,* comp. by Margery A. Ryerson (Philadelphia: J. B. Lippincott, 1923), p. 16.

6. Quoted in Rose Henderson, "Robert Henri," *The American Magazine of Art,* XXI (Jan., 1930), 10.

7. Quoted in *The Paintings of George Bellows* (New York: Alfred A. Knopf, 1929), p. x.

8. Quoted in Lloyd Goodrich, *John Sloan* (Published for the Whitney Museum of American Art. New York: Macmillan, 1952), p. 49.

9. Quoted in Van Wyck Brooks, *John Sloan* (New York: E. P. Dutton, 1955), p. 54.

10. From John Sloan, "Art Is, Was and Ever Will Be," as quoted in Oliver Sayler, *Revolt in the Arts* (New York: Brentano's, 1930), p. 319.

CHAPTER 10

1. *Max Weber* (New York: American Artists Group, Inc., 1945), not paged.

2. Laurence W. Chisolm, *Fenollosa: The Far East and American Culture* (New Haven: Yale University Press, 1963), p. 184.

3. Max Weber, "The Fourth Dimension from a Plastic Point of View," *Camera Work,* XXXI (July, 1910), 25.

4. Waldo Frank *et al.* (eds.), *America and Alfred Stieglitz* (New York: The Literary Guild, 1934), p. 4.

5. *Ibid.,* p. 245.

6. Quoted in Chisolm, *op. cit.,* p. 184.

7. Quoted in Lloyd Goodrich, *Max Weber* (Published for the Whitney Museum of American Art. New York: Macmillan, 1949), pp. 30–31.

8. William C. Agee, *Synchromism and Color Principles in American Painting* (New York: M. Knoedler & Co., 1965), p. 27.

9. John Marin, "John Marin By Himself," *Creative Arts,* III (Oct., 1928), xxvii.

10. Quoted in Frederick S. Wight, "John Marin—Frontiersman," *John Marin Memorial Exhibition* (New York: Whitney Museum of American Art, 1958), not paged.

11. Quoted in *Camera Work,* XLIII–XLIV (April–July, 1913), 18.

12. Quoted in Arthur Jerome Eddy, *Cubists and Post Impressionism* (Chicago: A. C. McClurg and Co., 1914), p. 48.

13. Quoted in Frederick S. Wight, *Arthur G. Dove* (Berkeley: University of California Press, 1958), p. 45.

14. Samuel M. Kootz, *Modern American Painters* (New York: Brewer and Warren, Inc., 1930), pp. 36–38.

15. Quoted in *Georgia O'Keeffe: Exhibition of Recent Paintings, 1935* (New York: An American Place Gallery, 1936), p. 4.

CHAPTER 11

1. Rhodes Johnson, "In Defense of Abstract Art," *Parnassus, XII* (Dec., 1940), 9–10, and *American Abstract Artists* (1938), *passim.* (A group of essays by AAA members.)

2. Quoted in Frederick S. Wight, "Charles Sheeler," *Art in America,* LXII (Oct., 1954), 199.

3. Edward Hopper, "Charles Burchfield," *The Arts,* XIV (July, 1928), 6–7.

4. Quoted in Henry Steele Commager, *The American Mind,* pp. 116–17.

5. Quoted in *Edward Hopper* (New York: The Museum of Modern Art, 1933), p. 17.

6. Quoted in Marcus Cunliffe, *The Literature of the United States,* p. 254.

7. Quoted in John I. H. Baur, *Philip Evergood* (Published for the Whitney Museum of American Art. New York: Praeger, 1960), p. 52.

8. George L. K. Morris, "The Quest for an Abstract Tradition," *Abstract American Artists* (1938), not paged.

9. Quoted in H. H. Arnason, *Stuart Davis Memorial Exhibition* (Washington: Smithsonian Institution, 1965), p. 42.

10. Quoted in Rudi Blesh, *Stuart Davis* (New York: Grove Press, 1960), p. 14.

11. Stuart Davis, "The Cube Root," *Art News,* XLI (Feb. 1, 1943), 34.

CHAPTER 12

1. *Art Digest,* XVI (Oct. 1, 1941), 5, 17.

2. Dore Ashton, *The Unknown Shore* (Boston: Little, Brown, 1962), p. 48. London: Studio Vista, 1964.

3. Harold Rosenberg, *The Anxious Object* (New York: Horizon Press, 1964), p. 40. London: Thames and Hudson, 1965.

4. Jean-Paul Sartre, *Existentialism,* trans. Bernard Frechtman (New York: Philosophical Library, 1947), pp. 37–38.

5. Ralph Waldo Emerson, *Nature, Addresses, and Lectures,* new and revised edition (Boston: Houghton, Mifflin and Company, 1883), pp. 103–4.

6. Mark Rothko and Adolph Gottlieb, Letter to the Art Editor, *The New York Times,* June 13, 1943, Section 2, p. 9.

7. Jackson Pollock, "My Painting," *Possibilities,* I (Winter, 1947–48), 79.

8. Harold Rosenberg, "The American Action Painters," *Art News,* LI (Dec., 1952), 22.

9. Mark Rothko, "The Romantics Were Prompted," *Possibilities,* I (Winter, 1947–48), 84.

10. Quoted in Eleanor C. Monro, "Figures to the Fore," *Horizon,* II (July, 1960), 114.

11. Ben. B. Seligman, *Most Notorious Victory: Man in an Age of Automation* (New York: The Free Press, 1966), 402.

12. Alan Solomon, *Robert Rauschenberg* (New York: The Jewish Museum, 1963), not paged.

13. Marshall McLuhan, *Understanding Media: The Extensions of Man* (New York: The New American Library, 1966), p. 20. London: Routledge & Kegan Paul, 1964.

14. Quoted in Barbara Rose (ed.), *Readings in American Art Since 1900* (New York: Frederick A. Praeger, 1968), p. 19.

15. Seligman, *op. cit.,* p. 374.

16. Quoted in G. R. Swenson, "What Is Pop Art?" *Art News,* LXII (Nov., 1963), 26, 63.

17. Quoted in Dore Ashton, "Al Held," *Studio International,* CXLVIII (Nov., 1964), 210.

18. Quoted in Bruce Glaser, Lucy Lippard (ed.), "Questions to Stella and Judd," *Art News,* LXV (Sept., 1966), 58.

Selected Bibliography

SURVEYS AND CRITICISM FROM THE NINETEENTH CENTURY

BENJAMIN, S. G. W. *Art in America: A Critical and Historical Sketch.* New York: Harper & Brothers, 1880.

DICKSON, HAROLD (ed.). *Observations on American Art: Selections from the Writings of John Neal (1793–1876).* State College, Pa.: Pennsylvania State College Studies, No. 12, 1943.

DUNLAP, WILLIAM. *A History of the Rise and Progress of the Arts of Design in the United States.* 2 vols. New York: 1834. Reissued ed. with additions by F. W. BAYLEY and C. E. GOODSPEED. 3 vols. Boston: 1918. Revised, enlarged ed. ALEXANDER WYCKOFF (ed.). Preface by WILLIAM P. CAMPBELL. 3 vols. New York: Blom, 1965.

JARVES, JAMES JACKSON. *The Art-Idea.* New York: Hurd and Houghton, 1864. Reissued, BENJAMIN ROWLAND, JR. (ed.). Cambridge, Mass.: Harvard University Press, 1960.

LESTER, C. EDWARDS. *The Artists of America.* New York: Baker & Scribner, 1846.

MONTGOMERY, WALTER (ed.). *American Art and American Art Collections.* 2 vols. Boston: E. W. Walker, 1889.

SHELDON, G. W. *American Painters.* New York: D. Appleton, 1879.

TUCKERMAN, HENRY T. *Artist-Life.* New York: D. Appleton, 1847.

———. *Book of the Artists.* New York: G. P. Putnam & Son, 1867.

SURVEYS AND CRITICISM FROM THE TWENTIETH CENTURY

BARKER, VIRGIL. *American Painting: History and Interpretation.* New York: Macmillan, 1950.

BAUR, JOHN I. H. *Revolution and Tradition in Modern American Art.* Cambridge, Mass.: Harvard University Press, 1951.

FLEXNER, JAMES THOMAS. *First Flowers of Our Wilderness: American Painting.* Boston: Houghton Mifflin, 1947.

———. *That Wilder Image.* Boston: Little, Brown, 1962.

———. *The Light of Distant Skies, 1760–1835.* New York: Harcourt, Brace, 1954.

GREENBERG, CLEMENT. *Art and Culture.* Boston: Beacon Press, 1961.

HARTMANN, SADAKICHI. *A History of American Art.* New rev. ed. 2 vols. New York: Tudor, 1934.

HESS, THOMAS B. *Abstract Painting: Background and American Phase.* New York: Viking Press, 1951.

McCoubrey, JOHN. *American Tradition in Painting.* New York: Braziller, 1963.

NOVAK, BARBARA. *American Painting of the Nineteenth Century.* New York: Praeger, 1969. London: Pall Mall Press, 1969.

RICHARDSON, E. P. *A Short History of Painting in America.* New York: Thomas Y. Crowell, 1963.

———. *Painting in America.* New York: Thomas Y. Crowell, 1956.

ROSE, BARBARA. *American Art Since 1900.* New York: Praeger, 1967. London: Thames and Hudson, 1968.

ANTHOLOGIES

The Artist in America. Compiled by the editors of *Art in America.* New York: W. W. Norton, 1967.

McCoubrey, JOHN. *American Art 1700–1960, Sources and Documents.* Englewood Cliffs, N.J.: Prentice-Hall, 1965.

RODMAN, SELDON. *Conversations with Artists.* New York: Devin-Adair, 1957.

ROSE, BARBARA. *Readings in American Art Since 1900.* New York: Praeger, 1968.

SPECIALIZED STUDIES

ASHTON, DORE. *The Unknown Shore: A View of Contemporary Art.* Boston: Little, Brown, 1962.

BORN, WOLFGANG. *American Landscape Painting.* New Haven, Conn.: Yale University Press, 1948.

———. *Still Life Painting in America.* New York: Oxford University Press, 1947.

BROWN, MILTON. *American Painting from the Armory Show to the Depression.* Princeton, N.J.: Princeton University Press, 1955.

DICKSON, HAROLD EDWARD. *Arts of the Young Republic: The Age of William Dunlap.* Chapel Hill: University of North Carolina Press, 1968.

DOVER, CEDRIC. *American Negro Art.* Greenwich, Conn.: The New York Graphic Society, 1960, 1969.

DRESSER, LOUISA (ed.), *XVIIth Century Painting in New England.* Worcester, Mass.: Worcester Art Museum, 1935.

FRANKENSTEIN, ALFRED. *After the Hunt: William Harnett and Other American Still Life Painters 1870–1900.* Rev. ed. Berkeley: University of California Press, 1969.

HARRIS, NEIL. *The Artist in American Society: The Formative Years 1790–1860.* New York: Braziller, 1966.

MILLER, LILLIAN B. *Patrons and Patriotism: The Encouragement of the Fine Arts in the United States 1790–1860.* Chicago: University of Chicago Press, 1966.

RICHARDSON, E. P. *American Romantic Painting.* New York: Weyhe, 1944.

Sears, Clara Endicott. *Highlights Among the Hudson River Artists.* Boston: Houghton Mifflin, 1947.

Tuchman, Maurice (ed.). *New York School: The First Generation, Paintings of the 1940's and 1950's.* Los Angeles: Los Angeles County Museum of Art, 1965. London: Thames and Hudson, 1971.

Wilmerding, John. *A History of American Marine Painting.* Salem, Mass.: Peabody Museum of Salem, and Boston: Little, Brown, 1968.

MONOGRAPHS

Bloch, E. Maurice. *George Caleb Bingham, The Evolution of an Artist. A Catalogue Raisonné.* 2 vols. Berkeley and Los Angeles: University of California Press, 1967.

Cikovsky, Nicolai, Jr. *George Inness.* New York: Praeger Publishers, 1971.

Cowdrey, Bartlett, and Williams, H. W., Jr. *William Sidney Mount, 1807–1868: An American Painter.* Published for The Metropolitan Museum of Art. New York: Columbia University Press, 1944.

Foote, Henry Wilder. *John Smibert.* Cambridge, Mass.: Harvard University Press, 1950.

Goodrich, Lloyd. *Thomas Eakins, His Life and Work.* New York: Whitney Museum of American Art, 1933.

———. *Winslow Homer.* New York: Published for the Whitney Museum of American Art. New York: Macmillan, 1944.

Goossen, E. C. *Stuart Davis.* New York: Braziller, 1959.

Hess, Thomas B. *Willem de Kooning.* New York: The Museum of Modern Art, 1968.

Homer, William Innes. *Robert Henri and His Circle.* Ithaca, N.Y.: Cornell University Press, 1969.

Prown, Jules David. *John Singleton Copley.* 2 vols. Cambridge, Mass.: Harvard University Press, 1966.

Richardson, E. P. *Washington Allston: A Study of the Romantic Artist in America.* Chicago: University of Chicago Press, 1948. New York: Apollo, 1967.

Rubin, William. *Stella.* New York: The Museum of Modern Art, 1970.

St. John, Bruce. *John Sloan.* New York: Praeger Publishers, 1971.

Sellers, Charles Coleman. *Charles Willson Peale.* New York: Charles Scribner's Sons, 1969.

List of Illustrations

Artists are listed in alphabetical order. All works are oil on canvas unless otherwise noted. Height precedes width. Numbers at the end of each entry indicate chapter and illustration.

ALLSTON, Washington (1779–1843)
Landscape with a Lake, 1804
38" x 51¼"
Courtesy, Museum of Fine Arts, Boston. M. and M. Karolik Collection   5–1

The Rising of a Thunderstorm at Sea, 1804
38½" x 51"
Courtesy, Museum of Fine Arts, Boston. M. and M. Karolik Collection   5–2

Portrait of William Ellery Channing, 1809–11
31⅛" x 27¾"
Courtesy, Museum of Fine Arts, Boston. Gift of William Francis Channing   5–3

Dead Man Restored to Life by Touching the Bones of the Prophet Elisha, 1811–13
156" x 132"
Courtesy of the Pennsylvania Academy of the Fine Arts, Philadelphia   5–4

Moonlit Landscape, 1819
24" x 35"
Courtesy, Museum of Fine Arts, Boston. Gift of Dr. W. S. Bigelow   5–5

The Spanish Girl in Reverie, 1831
30" x 25"
The Metropolitan Museum of Art, New York. Gift of Lyman G. Bloomingdale, 1901   5–7

American Scenery: Afternoon with a Southwest Haze, 1835
18½" x 24 2/5"
Courtesy, Museum of Fine Arts, Boston. Bequest of Edmund Dwight   5–6

ANONYMOUS
Dr. John Clark, ca. 1660's
34" x 27"
Courtesy of the Boston Medical Library in The Francis A. Countway Library of Medicine, Boston   1–1

Alice Mason, ca. 1670
33¼" x 24⅞"
Adams National Historic Site, National Park Service, U.S. Department of the Interior   1–4

Margaret Gibbs, 1670
40½" x 33"
Collection Mrs. David M. Giltinan. Photograph

courtesy Worcester Art Museum   1–6

John Freake, 1674
42½" x 36¾"
Worcester Art Museum. Sarah C. Garver Fund   1–3

Mrs. Elizabeth Freake and Baby Mary, ca. 1674
42½" x 36¾"
Worcester Art Museum. Gift of Mr. and Mrs. Albert W. Rice   1–5

John Wheelwright (?), 1677
30" x 25⅛"
Massachusetts Art Commission. Photograph courtesy Worcester Art Museum   1–2

Major Thomas Savage, 1679
42½" x 37⅛"
Collection Henry L. Shattuck. Photograph courtesy Worcester Art Museum   1–8

Pieter Schuyler, ca. 1690
86" x 48 1/5"
Collection Albany Institute of History and Art   1–12

Mrs. David Provoost, ca.
1700
Oil on panel, 30" x 24¾"
Courtesy of The New-York
Historical Society, New
York City   1–11

Portrait of John Van
Cortlandt, ca. 1731
57" x 41"
In the Brooklyn Museum
Collection   2–6

Phila Franks (Mrs. Oliver
DeLancey) and David
Franks, ca. 1735
44" x 34¾"
Captain N. Taylor Phillips,
U.S.A., Collection of the
American Jewish Historical
Society, Waltham, Mass.
Photograph courtesy of the
Frick Art Reference
Library   2–7

BADGER, Joseph (1708–65)
Mrs. Cassius Hunt, ca. 1760
49¾" x 39"
Courtesy of The New-York
Historical Society, New
York City   2–17

James Badger, 1760
42½" x 33⅛"
The Metropolitan Museum
of Art, New York. Rogers
Fund, 1929   2–19

BELLOWS, George (1882–
1925)
Stag at Sharkey's, 1907
36¼" x 48¼"
The Cleveland Museum of
Art. Hinman B. Hurlbut
Collection   9–7

The Lone Tenement, 1909
36⅛" x 48⅛"

National Gallery of Art,
Washington, D.C. Gift of
Chester Dale, 1962   9–8

Polo at Lakewood, 1910
45" x 63"
The Columbus Gallery of
Fine Arts, Columbus,
Ohio   9–10

Men of the Docks, 1912
45" x 63½"
Randolph-Macon Woman's
College, Lynchburg, Va.
                              9–9

Cliff Dwellers, 1913
39½" x 41½"
Los Angeles County Museum
of Art. Los Angeles County
Funds   9–6

Dempsey and Firpo, 1924
51" x 63¼"
Collection Whitney Museum
of American Art, New
York   9–11

BENTON, Thomas Hart
(1889–)
City Scenes, 1930
Oil on board, 77½" x 145½"
New School for Social
Research, New York   11–11

BIERSTADT, Albert (1830–
1902)
The Rocky Mountains, 1863
73½" x 120¾"
The Metropolitan Museum
of Art, New York. Rogers
Fund, 1907   7–12

BINGHAM, George Caleb
(1811–79)
Fur Traders Descending the
Missouri, 1845
29" x 36½"

The Metropolitan Museum
of Art, New York. Morris
K. Jessup Fund, 1933   6–18

Raftsmen Playing Cards,
1847
28" x 36"
City Art Museum of Saint
Louis. Gift of Ezra H.
Linley Fund   6–16

The County Election,
1851–52
35 7/16" x 48¾"
City Art Museum of Saint
Louis   6–14

Daniel Boone Escorting a
Band of Pioneers into the
Western Country, 1851–52
26" x 52"
Collection Washington
University, St. Louis   6–17

Order No. 11, 1869–70
56½" x 78"
The State Historical Society
of Missouri, Columbia, Mo.
                              6–19

BIRCH, Thomas (1779–
1851)
The "Wasp" and the "Fro-
lick," 1820
20" x 30"
Courtesy, Museum of Fine
Arts, Boston. M. and M.
Karolik Collection   5–16

BLACKBURN, Joseph (ac-
tive in New England 1753–
63)
The Winslow Family, 1757
42" x 102"
Courtesy, Museum of Fine
Arts, Boston. Abraham Shu-
man Collection   3–4

Mrs. Jonathan Warner,
ca. 1761
48¾" x 39"
Warner House, Portsmouth,
N.H. Photograph by Douglas Armsden, Kittery,
Maine   3–5

BRIDGES, Charles (born
ca. 1665)
Anne Byrd, 1735
50¼" x 40¼"
Colonial Williamsburg Collection, Williamsburg, Va.
                          2–4

Governor Alexander Spotswood, 1735–36
52" x 39½"
Colonial Williamsburg Collection, Williamsburg, Va.
                          2–5

CATLIN, George (1796–1872)
Big Elk, 1833
29" x 24"
Courtesy of National Collection of Fine Arts, Smithsonian Institution, Washington, D.C.   6–20

CÉZANNE, Paul (1839–1906)
Pines and Rocks, ca. 1904
32" x 25¾"
Collection, The Museum of Modern Art, New York.
Lillie P. Bliss Collection
                          8–13

CHANDLER, Winthrop
(1747–90)
Reverend Ebenezer Devotion, 1770
55" x 43¾"
Owned by the Brookline Historical Society, Brookline,

Mass. Photograph courtesy Museum of Fine Arts, Boston   3–6

CHURCH, Frederic Edwin
(1826–1900)
Floating Icebergs, 1859
Pencil and oil on cardboard,
6" x 10"
Courtesy of The Cooper-Hewitt Museum of Decorative Arts and Design, Smithsonian Institution, New
York   7–9

Twilight in the Wilderness,
1860
40" x 64"
The Cleveland Museum of Art. Mr. and Mrs. William H. Marlatt Fund   7–11

Cotopaxi, ca. 1863
35" x 60"
The Reading Public Museum and Art Gallery,
Reading, Pa.   7–10

COLE, Thomas (1801–48)
Expulsion from the Garden of Eden, ca. 1827–28
39" x 54"
Courtesy, Museum of Fine Arts, Boston. M. and M. Karolik Collection   6–3

*The Course of Empire:
Desolation,* 1836
39½" x 61"
Courtesy of The New-York Historical Society, New
York City   6–4

The Oxbow (the Connecticut River near Northampton),
1836
51½" x 76"
The Metropolitan Museum

of Art, New York. Gift of Mrs. Russell Sage, 1908
                          6–6

*Schroon Mountain,
Adirondacks,* 1838
39⅜" x 63"
The Cleveland Museum of Art. Hinman B. Hurlbut
Collection   6–13

The Architect's Dream, 1840
54" x 84"
The Toledo Museum of Art,
Toledo, Ohio. Gift of Florence Scott Libbey,
1949   6–5

View of the Falls of Munda near Portage on the Genesee Falls, New York, 1847
51" x 39½"
Museum of Art, Rhode Island School of Design,
Providence   6–8

COPLEY, John Singleton
(1738–1815)
Mrs. Joseph Mann, 1753
35 4/5" x 28 3/10"
Courtesy, Museum of Fine Arts, Boston. Gift of Frederick H. Metcalf and Holbrook E. Metcalf   3–9

Galatea, ca. 1754
37" x 52"
Courtesy, Museum of Fine Arts, Boston   3–8

Portrait of Theodore Atkinson, Jr., 1757
50" x 40"
Museum of Art, Rhode Island School of Design,
Providence   3–10

The Royall Sisters, ca. 1758

57½" x 48"
Courtesy, Museum of Fine Arts, Boston. Julia Knight Fox Fund 3–14

Epes Sargent, ca. 1760
49⅞" x 40"
National Gallery of Art, Washington, D. C. Gift of the Avalon Foundation 3–12

John Scollay, 1764
Pastel, 21⅞" x 16⅞"
Collection Mrs. Roland Greeley. Photograph courtesy Museum of Fine Arts, Boston 3–11

Mrs. John Powell, 1764
49½" x 39½"
Collection Ellery Sedgwick, Jr. Photograph courtesy of the Frick Art Reference Library 3–13

Portrait of Paul Revere, ca. 1768
34 4/5" x 28½"
Courtesy, Museum of Fine Arts, Boston. Gift of Joseph W. Revere, William B. and Edward H. R. Revere 3–15

Mrs. Ezekiel Goldthwait, 1770–71
50" x 39½"
Courtesy, Museum of Fine Arts, Boston. Bequest of John T. Bowen 3–2

Mrs. Thomas Gage, 1771
50" x 40"
Collection Viscount Gage. Photograph courtesy the Cortauld Institute of Art, London 3–16

Watson and the Shark, 1778
72" x 90 1/5"
Courtesy, Museum of Fine Arts, Boston. Gift of Mrs. George von Lengerke Meyer 4–4

The Collapse of the Earl of Chatham in the House of Lords, 1779–80
90" x 121"
The Tate Gallery, London 4–5

DAVIS, Stuart (1894–1964)
Lucky Strike, 1921
33¼" x 18"
Collection, The Museum of Modern Art, New York. Gift of The American Tobacco Company, Inc. 11–18

Town Square, 1925–26
Watercolor, 11¾" x 14¾"
Collection of The Newark Museum, Newark, New Jersey 11–19

Swing Landscape, 1938
84" x 168"
Courtesy of the Indiana University Art Museum, Bloomington 11–20

Visa, 1951
40" x 52"
Collection, The Museum of Modern Art, New York. Gift of Mrs. Gertrud A. Mellon 11–21

DE KOONING, Willem (1904–)
Painting, 1948
Enamel and oil on canvas, 42⅝" x 56⅛"
Collection, The Museum of Modern Art, New York 12–3

Woman I, 1950–52
75⅞" x 58"
Collection, The Museum of Modern Art, New York 12–5

Gotham News, ca. 1955
69" x 79"
Albright-Knox Art Gallery, Buffalo, N. Y. Gift of Seymour H. Knox 12–4

DEMUTH, Charles (1883–1935)
Modern Conveniences, 1921
25 7/16" x 20 15/16"
The Columbus Gallery of Fine Arts, Columbus, Ohio. Gift of Ferdinand Howald 11–2

Paquebot Paris, ca. 1922
24½" x 19 7/16"
The Columbus Gallery of Fine Arts, Columbus, Ohio. Gift of Ferdinand Howald 11–1

My Egypt, 1927
Oil on composition board, 35¾" x 30"
Collection Whitney Museum of American Art, New York 11–3

DIEBENKORN, Richard (1922–)
Woman in a Window, 1957
59" x 56"
Albright-Knox Art Gallery, Buffalo, N. Y. Gift of Seymour H. Knox 12–9

DOUGHTY, Thomas (1793–1856)
View of Baltimore from "Beach Hill," 1822
14¼" x 18¼"

Courtesy, Museum of Fine Arts, Boston. M. and M. Karolik Collection   6–2

DOVE, Arthur (1880–1946)
Plant Forms, 1915
Pastel on canvas,
17¼" x 23⅞"
Collection Whitney Museum of American Art, New York. Gift of Mr. and Mrs. Roy R. Neuberger   10–12

Sentimental Music, 1917
Pastel, 21¼" x 17⅞"
The Metropolitan Museum of Art. The Alfred Stieglitz Collection, 1949   10–11

Goin' Fishin', 1925
Collage, 19½" x 24"
The Phillips Collection, Washington, D.C.   10–13

Sunrise, Number 3, 1937
24⅞" x 35⅛"
Yale University Art Gallery, New Haven. Gift of the Collection Société Anonyme   10–14

DURAND, Asher B. (1796–1886)
Kindred Spirits, 1849
46" x 36"
Art and Architecture Division, The New York Public Library. Astor, Lenox and Tilden Foundations   6–7

In the Woods, 1855
60¾" x 48"
The Metropolitan Museum of Art, New York. Gift in memory of Jonathan Sturges by his children, 1895   6–9

DUVENECK, Frank (1848–1919)
Old Town Brook, Polling, Bavaria, ca. 1878
31" x 49"
Cincinnati Art Museum   8–2

DUYCKINCK, Gerret (1660–*ca.* 1712)
Self-Portrait, ca. 1700
Oil on panel, 30" x 25"
Courtesy of The New-York Historical Society, New York City   1–9

Mrs. Gerret Duyckinck, ca. 1700
Oil on panel, 30" x 25"
Courtesy of The New-York Historical Society, New York City   1–10

EAKINS, Thomas (1844–1916)
Max Schmitt in a Single Scull, 1871
32¼" x 46¼"
The Metropolitan Museum of Art, New York. Alfred N. Punnett Fund and gift of George D. Pratt, 1934   8–17

Starting Out After Rail, 1874
Watercolor, 25" x 20"
The Roland P. Murdock Collection. Wichita Art Museum, Wichita, Kansas   8–18

The Gross Clinic, 1875
96" x 78"
Courtesy of The Jefferson Medical College of Philadelphia. Photograph courtesy of the Philadelphia Museum of Art   8–19

The Swimming Hole, 1883
27" x 36"
Collection of the Fort Worth Art Center Museum   8–22

Between Rounds, 1899
50¼" x 40"
Collection of the Philadelphia Museum of Art   8–23

The Thinker: Louis N. Kenton, 1900
82" x 42"
The Metropolitan Museum of Art, New York. Kennedy Fund, 1917   8–20

Addie, 1900
24⅛" x 18¼"
Collection of the Philadelphia Museum of Art. Photograph by A. J. Wyatt, Staff photographer   8–21

EARL, Ralph (1751–1801)
Roger Sherman, ca. 1775–77
64⅜" x 49⅝"
Yale University Art Gallery, New Haven. Gift of Roger Sherman White   4–15

Portrait of Mrs. William Taylor, neé Abigail Starr, and her Child, Daniel Boardman, 1790
48½" x 38"
Albright-Knox Art Gallery, Buffalo, N. Y. Charles Clifton Fund   4–16

EVERGOOD, Philip (1901–   )
The Old Wharf, 1934
25 3/16" x 29½"
In the Brooklyn Museum Collection   11–15

276

Through the Mill, 1940
Oil and tempera on canvas,
36" x 52"
Collection Whitney Museum
of American Art, New York
11—16

FEKE, Robert (*ca.* 1706—
after 1750)
The Isaac Royall Family,
1741
56" x 78"
Harvard University Law
School, Cambridge, Mass.
2—13

Portrait of Josiah Martin, ca.
1748
50½" x 40¾"
The Toledo Museum of Art,
Toledo, Ohio. Gift of
Florence Scott Libbey, 1945
2—14

Mrs. Josiah Martin, ca. 1748
50½" x 40½"
Courtesy of The Detroit
Institute of Arts. Photo-
graph by Joseph Klima, Jr.
2—15

*Portrait of Mrs. James
Bowdoin II,* 1748
50⅛" x 40⅛"
Bowdoin College Museum of
Art, Brunswick, Maine
2—18

*Portrait of General Samuel
Waldo, ca.* 1748—50
96¾" x 60¼"
Bowdoin College Museum of
Art, Brunswick, Maine
2—16

GLACKENS, William
(1870—1938)
View of the East River from

Brooklyn, 1902
25¼" x 30"
Santa Barbara Museum of
Art. Preston Morton
Collection
9—15

The Drive, Central Park, ca.
1905
25¾" x 32"
The Cleveland Museum of
Art. Purchase from the
J. H. Wade Fund
9—18

Nude with Apple, 1910
40" x 57"
In The Brooklyn Museum
Collection
9—17

Beach Scene, New London,
1918
26" x 31⅞"
The Columbus Gallery of
Fine Arts, Columbus, Ohio.
Gift of Ferdinand Howald
9—19

GUY, Francis (*ca.* 1760—
1820)
Winter Scene in Brooklyn,
1817—20
58¾" x 75"
In The Brooklyn Museum
Collection
5—15

HARNETT, William Michael
(1848—92)
Music and Good Luck, 1888
40" x 30"
The Metropolitan Museum of
Art, New York. Catharine
Lorillard Wolfe Collection,
1963, Catherine Lorillard
Wolfe Fund
8—3

HEADE, Martin Johnson
(1819—1904)
Lake George, 1862
26" x 49¾"

Courtesy, Museum of Fine
Arts, Boston. M. and M.
Karolik Collection
7—7

HENRI, Robert (1865—1929)
The East River, New York,
ca. 1900—1905
26" x 32"
Courtesy Kennedy Galleries,
Inc., New York
9—1

West 57th Street, New York,
1902
26" x 32"
Yale University Art Gallery,
New Haven. The Mabel
Brady Garvan Collection
9—2

Dutch Joe, 1910
24" x 20 3/16"
Milwaukee Art Center
Collection
9—3

HESSELIUS, Gustavus
(1682—1755)
Mrs. Henry Darnall III, 1722
29⅝" x 25"
From the collections of The
Maryland Historical Society,
Baltimore
2—1

Bacchus and Ariadne, ca.
1720's
24½" x 32⅜"
The Detroit Institute of Arts
2—3

Mrs. Gustavus Hesselius, ca.
1740
36¼" x 28"
Courtesy of The Historical
Society of Pennsylvania,
Philadelphia
2—2

HOFMANN, Hans (1880—
1966)

277

Smaragd Red and Germinating Yellow, 1959
55" x 40"
Contemporary Collection of The Cleveland Museum of Art   12–6

HOMER, Winslow (1836–1910)
Long Branch, New Jersey, 1869
16" x 21¾"
Courtesy, Museum of Fine Arts, Boston. Charles Henry Hayden Fund   8–8

Two Guides, 1876
24" x 38½"
Sterling and Francine Clark Art Institute, Williamstown, Mass.   8–9

The Fog Warning, 1885
30" x 48"
Courtesy, Museum of Fine Arts, Boston. Otis Norcrosse Fund   8–11

Hunter in the Adirondacks, 1892
Watercolor, 13¼" x 19½"
Courtesy of the Fogg Art Museum, Harvard University, Cambridge, Mass.
Anonymous gift   8–12

The Fox Hunt, 1893
38" x 68"
Courtesy of the Pennsylvania Academy of the Fine Arts, Philadelphia   8–14

Northeaster, 1895
34⅜" x 50¼"
The Metropolitan Museum of Art, New York. Gift of George A. Hearn, 1910
8–15

After the Hurricane, Bahamas, ca. 1898–99
Watercolor, 14 5/16" x 21⅜"
Courtesy of The Art Institute of Chicago   8–10

The Gulf Stream, 1899
28⅛" x 49⅛"
The Metropolitan Museum of Art, New York. Wolfe Fund, 1906   8–16

HOPPER, Edward (1882–1967)
House by the Railroad, 1925
24" x 29"
Collection, The Museum of Modern Art, New York
11–6

Sunday, 1926
29" x 34"
The Phillips Collection, Washington, D.C.   11–8

Room in New York, 1932
29" x 36"
F. M. Hall Collection, University of Nebraska Art Galleries, Lincoln, Nebraska
11–7

HUNT, William Morris (1824–79)
The Little Gleaner, 1854
54" x 38"
The Toledo Museum of Art, Toledo, Ohio. Gift of Arthur J. Secor, 1923
7–13

INNESS, George (1825–94)
The Sun Shower, 1847
30⅛" x 42⅛"
Santa Barbara Museum of Art. Preston Morton Collection   7–17

On the Delaware River, 1873
28⅜" x 48¼"
In the Brooklyn Museum Collection   7–20

Autumn Landscape, October, 1886
Oil on panel, 20" x 30"
Los Angeles County Museum of Art. The Paul Rodman Mabury Collection   7–18

The Afterglow, 1893
32" x 25¼"
Courtesy of The Art Institute of Chicago   7–19

JARVIS, John Wesley (1780–1840)
Commodore Oliver Perry at the Battle of Lake Erie, 1816
96" x 60"
Courtesy, Art Commission of The City of New York
5–17

JOHNSON, Eastman (1824–1906)
Old Kentucky Home, 1859
36" x 45"
Courtesy of The New-York Historical Society, New York City   7–14

Woman on a Hill, ca. 1870
25¾" x 21¼"
Addison Gallery of American Art, Phillips Academy, Andover, Mass.   7–16

The Nantucket School of Philosophy, 1887
Oil on panel, 23¼" x 31¾"
Courtesy, Walters Art Gallery, Baltimore   7–15

KELLY, Ellsworth (1923–)

Red Blue, 1962
90" x 69½"
Contemporary Collection of
The Cleveland Museum of
Art   12–15

KENSETT, John Frederick
(1816–72)
English Landscape, ca.
1843–45
Oil on academy board,
12" x 14"
In The Brooklyn Museum
Collection. Gift of Mrs.
Charles D. Childs   7–3

High Bank, Genesee River,
1857
30½" x 49¼"
In the collection of The
Corcoran Gallery of Art,
Washington, D.C.   7–4

Lake George, 1869
44⅛" x 66⅜"
The Metropolitan Museum
of Art, New York. Bequest
of Maria De Witt Jesup, 1915
                        7–5

Third Beach, Newport, 1869
11⅝" x 24¼"
Courtesy of The Art Institute
of Chicago   7–6

KNELLER, Sir Godfrey
(*ca.* 1646–1723)
Princess Ann of Denmark,
1692
Mezzotint by I. Smith
Courtesy, The Henry Francis
du Pont Winterthur Mu-
seum, Winterthur Delaware
                       2–11

KRIMMEL, John Lewis
(1789–1821)
Interior of an American Inn,

ca. 1813
16⅞" x 22½"
The Toledo Museum of Art,
Toledo, Ohio. Gift of
Florence Scott Libbey, 1954
                        5–14

LANE, Fitz Hugh
(1804–65)
*Owl's Head, Penobscot
Bay, Maine,* 1862
16" x 26"
Courtesy, Museum of Fine
Arts, Boston. M. and M.
Karolik Collection   7–8

LEUTZE, Emanuel Gottlieb
(1816–68)
*Washington Crossing the
Delaware,* 1851
149" x 256"
The Metropolitan Museum
of Art, New York. Gift of
John S. Kennedy, 1897
                        7–1

LICHTENSTEIN, Roy
(1923–)
Good Morning Darling, 1964
Magna on canvas, 27" x 36"
Collection David Lichten-
stein. Photograph courtesy
Leo Castelli Gallery, New
York   12–13

LUKS, George (1867–1933)
The Old Duchess, 1905
30" x 25"
The Metropolitan Museum
of Art, New York. George
A. Hearn Fund, 1921
                        9–4

The Spielers, 1905
36" x 26"
Addison Gallery of Ameri-
can Art, Phillips Academy,
Andover, Mass.   9–5

MACDONALD-WRIGHT,
Stanton (1890–)
*"Oriental." Synchromy in
Blue-Green,* 1918
36" x 50"
Collection Whitney Museum
of American Art, New York
                       10–5

MARIN, John (1870–1951)
Brooklyn Bridge, 1910
Watercolor, 18½" x 15½"
The Metropolitan Museum
of Art, New York. The
Alfred Stieglitz Collection,
1949   10–7

Lower Manhattan, 1920
Watercolor, 21⅞" x 26¾"
Collection, The Museum of
Modern Art, New York.
The Philip L. Goodwin
Collection   10–8

*Pertaining to Stonington
Harbor, Maine, no. 4,* 1926
Watercolor, 15⅝" x 21¾"
The Metropolitan Museum
of Art, New York. The
Alfred Stieglitz Collection,
1949   10–9

Lobster Boat, 1940
22" x 28"
Private collection. Photograph by Charles Uht
                      10–10

MORRIS, George L. K.
(1905–)
Nautical Composition,
1937–42
51" x 35"
Collection Whitney Museum
of American Art, New York
                      11–17

279

MORSE, Samuel F. B.
(1791–1872)
*The Old House of Represen-
tatives,* 1822
86½" x 130¾"
In the collection of The
Corcoran Gallery of Art,
Washington, D.C.   5–12

Lafayette, 1826
96" x 64"
Courtesy, Art Commission
of The City of New York
                          5–11

MOUNT, William Sidney
(1807–68)
Dancing on the Barn Floor,
1831
25" x 30"
Suffolk Museum and Car-
riage House, Stony Brook,
New York. Melville
Collection   6–15

Bargaining for a Horse, 1835
24" x 30"
Courtesy of The New-York
Historical Society, New York
City   6–10

Eel Spearing at Setauket,
1845
29" x 36"
New York State Historical
Association, Cooperstown
                        6–12

The Bone Player, 1856
36¼" x 29"
Courtesy, Museum of Fine
Arts, Boston. M. and M.
Karolik Collection   6–11

NOLAND, Kenneth
(1924–)
Morning Span, 1963
Acrylic on canvas,

103¾" x 142½"
Courtesy of the André
Emmerich Gallery, New
York   12–18

Royal Drawl, 1970
Acrylic on canvas,
62½" x 114"
Courtesy of the Lawrence
Rubin Gallery, New York
                        12–16

O'KEEFFE, Georgia
(1887–)
Black Iris, 1926
36" x 29⅞"
The Metropolitan Museum
of Art, New York. The
Alfred Stieglitz Collection,
on loan from Georgia
O'Keeffe; 1949   10–15

PEALE, Charles Willson
(1741–1827)
*George Washington (at
Princeton),* 1779
93" x 58½"
Courtesy of the Pennsylvania
Academy of the Fine Arts,
Philadelphia   4–17

Staircase Group, 1795
89" x 39½"
Philadelphia Museum of
Art. George W. Elkins
Collection   4–18

*Exhuming the First
American Mastodon,*
1806–8
50" x 62"
The Peale Museum, Balti-
more. Gift of Mrs. Harry
White in memory of her
husband   4–19

Hannah Moore Peale, 1816
24⅛" x 20½"

Courtesy, Museum of Fine
Arts, Boston. Gift of Mrs.
Reginald Seabury Parker in
memory of her husband
                        4–20

PEALE, Raphaelle
(1774–1825)
After the Bath, 1823
29" x 24"
Nelson Gallery–Atkins Mu-
seum (Nelson Fund),
Kansas City, Mo.   5–13

PETO, John F. (1854–1907)
Old Time Letter Rack, 1894
30" x 25"
Courtesy, Museum of Fine
Arts, Boston. Bequest of
Maxim Karolik   8–4

POLLOCK, Jackson
(1912–56)
Guardians of the Secret,
1943
48" x 76"
San Francisco Museum of
Art. The Albert M. Bender
Bequest Fund   12–2

Cathedral, 1947
Mixed media on canvas,
71½" x 35 1/16"
Dallas Museum of Fine Arts.
Gift of Mr. and Mrs. Bernard
J. Reis   12–1

PRENDERGAST, Maurice
(1859–1924)
The East River, 1901
Watercolor, 13¾" x 19¾"
Collection, The Museum of
Modern Art, New York.
Gift of Abby Aldrich
Rockefeller   10–1

The Flying Horses, 1908–9
23⅞" x 32⅛"

The Toledo Museum of Art, Toledo, Ohio. Florence Scott Libbey Bequest, 1957
10–2

QUIDOR, John (1801–81)
Ichabod Crane Pursued by the Headless Horseman, 1828
22⅛" x 30 1/6"
Yale University Art Gallery, New Haven. The Mabel Brady Garvan Collection 6–1

RAUSCHENBERG, Robert (1925–)
White Painting (7 panels), 1951
House paint on canvas, 72" x 126"
Collection the artist   12–10

Gloria, 1956
Oil and paper collage on canvas, 66¼" x 63¼"
The Cleveland Museum of Art. Gift of The Cleveland Society for Contemporary Art   12–11

RAY, Man (1890–)
The Rope Dancer Accompanies Herself with Her Shadows, 1916
52" x 73⅜"
Collection, The Museum of Modern Art, New York. Gift of G. David Thompson
10–17

ROTHKO, Mark (1903–70)
Baptismal Scene, 1945
Watercolor, 19⅞" x 14"
Collection Whitney Museum of American Art, New York
12–7

Red Maroons 1962 #2, 1962
79" x 81"

Contemporary Collection and Friends of The Cleveland Museum of Art   12–8

RUSSELL, Morgan (1886–1953)
Synchromy, 1914–15
13" x 13¾"
Collection Benjamin F. Garber, New York   10–6

RYDER, Albert Pinkham (1847–1917)
Toilers of the Sea, before 1884
Oil on panel, 11½" x 12"
The Metropolitan Museum of Art, New York. George A. Hearn Fund, 1915   8–5

Jonah, ca. 1890
26½" x 33½"
Courtesy of National Collection of Fine Arts, Smithsonian Institution, Washington, D.C. Gift of John Gellatly   8–7

Moonlit Cove, ca. 1890–1900
14" x 17"
The Phillips Collection, Washington, D.C.   8–6

SCHAMBERG, Morton L. (1882–1918)
Telephone, 1916
24" x 20"
The Columbus Gallery of Fine Arts, Columbus, Ohio. Gift of Ferdinand Howald
10–16

SHAHN, Ben (1898–1969)
The Passion of Sacco and Vanzetti, 1931–32
Tempera on canvas, 84½" x 48"
Collection Whitney Museum

of American Art, New York. Gift of Mr. and Mrs. Milton Lowenthal in memory of Juliana Force   11–14

Scott's Run, West Virginia, 1937
Tempera on cardboard, 22¼" x 27⅞"
Collection Whitney Museum of American Art, New York
11–12

Mural in the Community Center, Roosevelt, New Jersey, 1937–38
Fresco, 12' x 45'
From James Thrall Soby, *Ben Shahn: Paintings.* New York: George Braziller, 1963. Photo Meyer   11–13

SHEELER, Charles (1883–1965)
Interior, 1926
33" x 22"
Collection Whitney Museum of American Art, New York
11–5

American Landscape, 1930
24" x 31"
Collection, The Museum of Modern Art, New York. Gift of Abby Aldrich Rockefeller   11–4

SLOAN, John (1871–1951)
Three A. M., 1909
32" x 26"
Collection of the Philadelphia Museum of Art. Photograph by Alfred J. Wyatt
9–16

Woman's Work, ca. 1911
31⅛" x 25¾"
The Cleveland Museum of

Art. Gift of Amelia Elizabeth
White 9–12

Little Movie Theater, 1913
20" x 24"
The Toledo Museum of Art,
Toledo, Ohio. Museum
Purchase, 1940 9–13

The White Way, 1926
30" x 32"
Collection of the Philadelphia Museum of Art. Photograph by Alfred J. Wyatt
9–14

SMIBERT, John (1688–1751)
The Bermuda Group, 1729
69½" x 93"
Yale University Art Gallery,
New Haven. Gift of Isaac
Lothrop of Plymouth, Mass.
2–8

Mrs. Daniel Oliver, ca. 1731
50" x 39½"
Collection Andrew Oliver.
Photograph courtesy of the
Frick Art Reference Library
2–10

Mrs. John Erving, ca. 1732
39¾" x 30¾"
Collection James Gore King.
Photograph courtesy of the
Frick Art Reference Library
2–9

Sir Richard Spry, ca. 1746
49½" x 39½"
Portsmouth Athenaeum,
Portsmouth, N.H. Photo-
graph courtesy of the Frick
Art Reference Library
2–12

SMITH, Captain Thomas
(active *ca.* 1675–1700)

Self-Portrait, ca. 1690
24½" x 23¾"
Worcester Art Museum
1–7

STELLA, Frank (1936–)
Gran Cairo, 1962
Synthetic polymer paint on
canvas, 85½" x 85½"
Collection Whitney Museum
of American Art, New York.
Gift of the Friends of the
Whitney Museum of Amer-
ican Art 12–17

STUART, Gilbert (1755–
1828)
The Skater, 1782
96⅛" x 58⅛"
National Gallery of Art,
Washington, D.C. Andrew
Mellon Collection 4–10

George Washington
(Vaughan Portrait), 1795
29" x 23¾"
National Gallery of Art,
Washington, D.C. Andrew
Mellon Collection 4–11

Mrs. Thomas Lea, ca. 1798
28" x 22"
Collection Lea Shippen
Luquer. Photograph courtesy
of the Frick Art Reference
Library 4–12

Thomas Jefferson, 1799
48⅛" x 39¾"
Bowdoin College Museum
of Art, Brunswick, Maine
4–13

*Reverend William Ellery
Channing,* ca. 1825
29¼" x 24½" (sight)
Private collection, New York
4–14

TRUMBULL, John
(1756–1843)
Battle of Bunker's Hill, 1785
25" x 34"
Yale University Art Gallery,
New Haven. 4–6

*General George Washington
Before the Battle of Trenton,*
after 1792
26½" x 18½"
The Metropolitan Museum
of Art, New York. Bequest
of Grace Wilkes, 1922
4–8

*View of Niagara on the
British Side,* 1807
24¼" x 36⅞"
Courtesy, Wadsworth
Atheneum, Hartford 4–9

*The Surrender of Lord Corn-
wallis at Yorktown, Virginia,
19 October, 1781,* 1824
12' x 18'
Rotunda of the Capitol,
Washington, D.C. Photo-
graph courtesy of The Li-
brary of Congress 4–7

VANDERLYN, John
(1775–1852)
The Death of Jane McCrea,
1804
32½" x 26½"
Courtesy, Wadsworth
Atheneum, Hartford 5–8

*Ariadne Asleep on the Island
of Naxos,* 1814
68" x 87"
Courtesy of the Pennsylvania
Academy of the Fine Arts,
Philadelphia 5–9

Versailles (detail), 1816–19
12' x 165'

The Metropolitan Museum of Art. Gift of the Senate House Association, Kingston, New York, 1952   5–10

WARHOL, Andy (1930–)
Campbell Soup Can 19¢,
1960
72" x 54½"
Collection Mr. and Mrs. Robert A. Rowan. Photograph courtesy Pasadena Art Museum   12–12

Elvis, 1964
Acrylic and silkscreen enamel on canvas, 82" x 60"
Collection Leo Castelli Gallery, New York   12–14

WEBER, Max (1881–1961)
Chinese Restaurant, 1915
40" x 48"
Collection Whitney Museum of American Art, New York   10–4

Adoration of the Moon, 1944
48" x 32"
Collection Whitney Museum of American Art, New York   10–3

WEST, Benjamin (1738–1820)

Landscape with Cow, ca. 1750
Oil on board, 26" x 49½"
Courtesy of the Pennsylvania Hospital, Philadelphia   3–7

Thomas Mifflin as a Boy, ca. 1758
51½ x 38½"
The Historical Society of Pennsylvania, Philadelphia   3–1

The Death of Wolfe, 1770
59½" x 84"
The National Gallery of Canada, Ottawa. Canadian War Memorials Collection   4–1

Saul and the Witch of Endor, 1777
19 15/16" x 25¾"
Courtesy, Wadsworth Atheneum, Hartford   4–2

Death on the Pale Horse, 1802
21" x 36"
Collection of the Philadelphia Museum of Art   4–3

WHISTLER, James A. McNeil (1834–1903)
Purple and Rose: The

Lange Lijzen of the Six Marks, 1864
35 4/5" x 22"
Courtesy of the John G. Johnson Collection, Philadelphia   8–1

WOLLASTON, John (active in America 1749–58)
Mrs. William Walton, ca. 1750
50" x 40"
Courtesy of The New-York Historical Society, New York City   3–3

WOOD, Grant (1892–1942)
American Gothic, 1930
Oil on panel, 29⅞" x 24⅞"
Courtesy of The Art Institute of Chicago   11–10

Daughters of Revolution, 1932
20" x 40"
Cincinnati Art Museum, courtesy Associated American Artists, New York   11–9

WOODVILLE, Richard Caton (1825–56)
The Sailor's Wedding, 1852
18½" x 22"
Courtesy Walters Art Gallery, Baltimore   7–2

Index

Abstract Expressionism, 238, 240–42, 247, 251, 257, 260
Albers, Josef, 239
Allston, Washington, 32, 65, 87–90, 92, 94, 96, 100, 102, 110, 128, 148–49, 212, 249–50
American Abstract Artists, 234
American Academy of Fine Arts, 88, 101
American Art-Union, 129
American Artists Congress, 229
"American Scholar, The" (Emerson), 241–42
Anshutz, Thomas, 178
Apollo Association, 129
Armory Show (1913), 176, 186, 194
Association of American Painters and Sculptors, 194
Austin, Darrel, 153

Badger, Joseph, 24, 33, 42, 45, 51, 53
Barbizon School, 110, 140, 144, 146, 152, 175
Baroque style, 11, 17, 19, 29, 45, 66
Bartram, William, 75
Baudelaire, Charles, 118
Baur, John I. H., 134
Beecher, Henry Ward, 164
Bellows, George, 180, 184, 186, 188, 196, 238, 242
Benton, Thomas Hart, 148, 215, 227–29, 234, 238, 242
Berkeley, George, 32, 42, 63
Bierstadt, Albert, 129, 140
Bingham, George Caleb, 107, 118, 120–21, 123, 125, 129, 131, 137, 225, 228

Birch, Thomas, 102, 135
Blackburn, Joseph, 32, 45, 48–49, 55–56
Blakelock, Ralph, 156
Breton, André, 240
Bridges, Charles, 29, 32
Brown, Charles Brockden, 88
Bryant, William Cullen, 114, 137
Burchfield, Charles, 148, 222
Burke, Edmund, 68

Cassatt, Mary, 150
Catlin, George, 125–26
Centennial Exposition (1876), 150
Cézanne, Paul, 164, 194, 198, 201–2, 205, 251
Chandler, Winthrop, 49
Channing, William Ellery, 88
Chase, William Merritt, 222
Chirico, Giorgio di, 237
Church, Frederic Edwin, 136–38, 140, 144, 146
Civil War, 128, 131, 140, 143, 150, 152, 158
Clark, John, 11, 13
Cole, Thomas, 60, 94, 107–12, 114, 116, 123, 126, 128, 136, 138, 146, 161, 164, 223, 247
Coleridge, Samuel Taylor, 75, 90, 156
Columbianum, 88
Cooper, James Fenimore, 107, 109, 118
Copley, John Singleton, 24, 26, 32–33, 36, 44–45, 49, 51, 53–57, 60–65, 68, 70–71, 73, 76, 87, 168, 194
Courbet, Gustave, 150
Crane, Stephen, 165, 178

Cubism, 193–94, 198, 200–201, 205, 207, 213, 220, 228, 236, 239, 242, 245
Cubo-Futurism, 218
Cunliffe, Marcus, 108
Curry, John Steuart, 227

Dada, 212–14, 237
David, Jacques-Louis, 51
Davis, Arthur B., 176
Davis, Stuart, 234, 236–39, 259
De Kooning, Willem, 245–47, 252
Demuth, Charles, 216, 218, 220, 222
Diebenkorn, Richard, 251
Doughty, Thomas, 107, 110
Dove, Arthur, 194, 197–98, 208–9, 211–12
Dow, Arthur, 198
Dreiser, Theodore, 178, 223
Duchamp, Marcel, 212–13, 218, 229
Durand, Asher B., 107, 109–10, 114, 116, 118–19, 128, 131, 136, 222
Durand, John, 49
Düsseldorf Gallery, 129, 136
Düsseldorf School, 129, 136, 140, 143
Duveneck, Frank, 178
Duyckinck, Gerret, 19, 21
Dyck, Anthony van, 10, 32

Eakins, Thomas, 55, 61, 76, 152–53, 163, 167–69, 171, 173, 175, 178
Earl, Ralph, 43, 65, 75, 82, 135, 168, 222, 239
Eight, The, 176, 180, 187–88, 196
Emerson, Ralph Waldo, 106, 109, 112, 212, 241
Emmons, Nathaniel, 24
Evergood, Philip, 232
Existentialism, 241
Expressionism, 194, 198, 200

Fauvism, 194, 197–98, 200, 205, 236, 251
Federal Art Project of the WPA, 216
Feke, Robert, 24, 32–33, 36, 38, 42, 45, 49, 51, 53, 55–56, 62
Fenollosa, Ernest, 195, 198
Fiske, John, 164

Flexner, James Thomas, 30
Foster, John, 11
Franklin, Benjamin, 89
Fuller, George, 156
Fuller, Robert, 96
Futurism, 194, 198, 205

Garland, Hamlin, 165
Gérôme, Jean-Léon, 168
Glackens, William, 176–77, 188, 190, 193, 196
Gottlieb, Adolph, 60, 242
Goya, Francisco, 51
Graves, Morris, 153
Greenwood, Joseph, 45, 53
Guy, Francis, 102, 107, 110, 119

Hambridge, Jay, 186
Hard Edge art, 257
Harnett, William, 152–53
Hawthorne, Nathaniel, 10
Heade, Martin Johnson, 135–36
Held, Al, 257
Henri, Robert, 150, 176–78, 180, 196, 205, 215, 222
Hesselius, Gustavus, 23, 25–26, 29, 33, 49, 51
Hesselius, John, 29, 45
Hofmann, Hans, 234, 247
Homer, Winslow, 55, 152–53, 158–61, 163–65, 167–69, 175, 184, 205
Hopper, Edward, 215, 222–23, 225, 228, 232
Hudson, Thomas, 45
Hudson River School, 98, 107, 109–10, 114, 120, 131, 138, 140, 146, 148, 150, 158, 161, 163, 227, 237, 245
Humboldt, Alexander von, 138
Hunt, William Morris, 129, 140
Hutchinson, Anne, 17

Impressionism, 114, 149, 152, 159, 176, 188, 190, 251
Inness, George, 142, 144, 146, 148–49, 153, 156
Irving, Washington, 88, 106

James, Henry, 135, 160

Jarvis, John Wesley, 102, 131
Jefferson, Thomas, 71, 108
Johnson, Eastman, 129, 142–44, 146, 158–59, 227
Johnson, Henrietta, 23

Kandinsky, Wassily, 254
Kelly, Ellsworth, 257
Kensett, John Frederick, 43, 131, 134, 136, 144, 146
Kneller, Godfrey, 24, 29, 33, 42
Krimmell, John Lewis, 102
Kroll, Leon, 190
Kühn, Justus Englehardt, 23

La Farge, John, 152
Lane, Fitz Hugh, 135–36
Lawson, Ernest, 176
"Letters on Landscape Painting" (Durand), 116
Leutze, Emanuel, 129, 225
Logan, James, 26
Lorrain, Claude, 92
Luks, George, 176–78, 180, 188
Luminist style, 134–37, 237–38

McCrea, Jane, 98
Macdonald-Wright, Stanton, 200–202
Manet, Edouard, 160, 168, 178, 184
Marin, John, 194–95, 197, 202, 205, 207–8, 229, 238
Masson, André, 240
Matisse, Henri, 176, 196, 239
Mengs, Anton Raphael, 66
Minimal art, 257
Mondrian, Piet, 205, 240, 257
Morris, George L. K., 234
Morse, Samuel F. B., 65, 87–88, 92, 100–102, 114, 128, 168, 216
Mount, William Sidney, 107, 118–20, 131, 137, 228
Munich School, 152
Myers, Jerome, 176–77

Nabis, 196–97
National Academy of Design, 100, 118, 149
Neal, John, 107

Neo-Impressionism, 200, 203
Noland, Kenneth, 257, 259–60
Non-Objectivists, 240
Norris, Frank, 165, 177–78

O'Keeffe, Georgia, 195, 197, 212
Oldenburg, Claes, 254
Op art, 257
Orozco, José Clemente, 229, 242
Orphism, 200–201, 236

Page, William, 96
Patroon Painters, 30
Peale, Charles Willson, 32, 62, 65, 67, 72, 83, 85, 86, 89, 102, 168
Peale, Raphaelle, 102
Peale, Rembrandt, 85
Pelham, Peter, 53
Pennsylvania Academy of the Fine Arts, 88, 167, 178, 222
Peto, John F., 152–53
Philadelphia School of Industrial Arts, 220
Picabia, Francis, 212, 229
Picasso, Pablo, 176, 184, 198
Poe, Edgar Allan, 94
Pollock, Jackson, 242, 244–45, 247, 249, 257
Pop art, 43, 190, 254, 257
Post–Civil War, 142
Post-Impressionism, 176, 190, 200
Pratt, Matthew, 45
Precisionists (Immaculates, Cubist-Realists), 216, 218
Prendergast, Maurice, 176, 190, 196–97, 205

Quidor, John, 106

Raphael, 66, 89, 94, 100–102
Rauschenberg, Robert, 252, 254, 257
Ray, Man, 213
Regionalism, 227, 232
Rembrandt, 9, 143
Renaissance, 94, 100, 201, 246
Renoir, Pierre Auguste, 188, 190
Revolutionary War, 24, 29, 32, 45, 61–65, 71, 83, 88, 98, 105

Reynolds, Joshua, 51, 55, 60, 66, 76
Richardson, E. P., 89
Rimmer, William, 96
Rivera, Diego, 229
Rococo style, 45, 55
Roosevelt, Theodore, 177, 195
Rosenberg, Harold, 241, 244
Rothko, Mark, 242, 247, 249–50
Royal Academy, 66
Royall, Isaac, 36, 42
Russell, Morgan, 200–202
Ryder, Albert Pinkham, 152–53, 156,
    158, 163, 209

Sargent, John Singer, 150
Sartre, Jean-Paul, 241
Schamberg, Morton, 212–13
Schwitters, Kurt, 237
Seurat, Georges, 200, 251
Shahn, Ben, 215, 232, 234
Shaw, Joshua, 107
Sheeler, Charles, 216, 218, 220
Shinn, Everett, 176–77
Sloan, John, 176–77, 186–88, 196
Smibert, John, 26, 29, 32–33, 36, 42,
    48, 53, 63, 78
Smith, Captain Thomas, 13, 16–17
Social Realists, 229, 232, 238
Society of American Artists, 149, 153,
    156, 164
Society of Artists, 60
Stella, Frank, 257–59
Stieglitz, Alfred, 150, 195, 197–98, 211,
    214
Stuart, Gilbert, 64–65, 76, 78, 82, 98
Sully, Thomas, 102
Surrealism, 150, 211 237, 240, 242
Swedenborg, Emanuel, 146
Synchromism, 200–202, 205, 228
Synthetic Cubism, 198

Thornhill, James, 32
Titian, 90, 92
Transcendentalism, 88, 109
Treasury Department Section of Paint-
    ing and Sculpture, 216
Trumbull, John, 32, 65, 71–73, 75–76,
    78, 87, 90, 101–2, 107, 216
Tuckerman, Henry T., 129, 134

Unitarianism, 88
Universal Exposition in Paris (1867),
    160, 168

Vanderlyn, John, 65, 87, 90, 96, 98,
    100, 102, 128
Vedder, Elihu, 152
Venetian painting, 90
Vuillard, Jean Edouard, 196

Walkowitz, Abraham, 195
Walpole, Horace, 68
War of 1812, 101, 105
Warhol, Andy, 254
Watson, John, 24
Weber, Max, 194–96, 198, 200, 205
Wesselmann, Tom, 190
West, Benjamin, 44–45, 51, 53, 55, 60,
    64–68, 70–71, 73, 76, 78, 83, 87, 89,
    150, 194
Whistler, James A. McNeill, 150, 178,
    203
Whitman, Walt, 137, 212, 242
Whittredge, Worthington, 129
Winckelmann, Johann, 65
Wissing, William, 33
Wollaston, John, 29, 32–33, 45, 48, 51
Wood, Grant, 223, 225, 227
Woodville, Richard Caton, 129, 131
World War I, 200, 215–16, 228
World War II, 150, 215, 239